MODERN
Witch

Devin Hunter has been initiated in several occult traditions. He's the founder of Sacred Fires, his own spiritual tradition, and is the cofounder of the Black Rose Tradition of Witchcraft. He has been serving clients all over the world for almost two decades through his work as a professional psychic-medium and occultist and through the Mystic Dream, his store in Walnut Creek, California. Devin hosts an AV Club–favorited podcast and publishes the magazine *Modern Witch*.

**LLEWELLYN
PUBLICATIONS**
woodbury, minnesota

DEVIN HUNTER

MODERN
Witch

SPELLS,
RITUALS,
and
WORKINGS

FIRST EDITION
Second Printing, 2020

Book design by Rebecca Zins
Cover design by Llewellyn Art Department
Cover photography by Ellen Lawson
Photographs and illustrations by Devin Hunter except
photo on page v, wheel on page 61, and Seal of Jupiter on page 214
Universal Tarot cards reproduced by permission of Lo Scarabeo,
© Massimiliano Filadoro; art by Roberto De Angelis

Llewellyn is a registered trademark of Llewellyn Worldwide Ltd.

Library of Congress Cataloging-in-Publication Data
Names: Hunter, Devin, author.
Title: Modern witch : spells, recipes, and workings / Devin Hunter.
Description: First edition. | Woodbury : Llewellyn Worldwide. Ltd, 2020. |
    Includes bibliographical references. | Summary: "The color photos
    throughout this book depict actual spells in progress so you can get a
    better understanding of what makes magic successful, an especially
    important feature for visual learners and for those who want to express
    their passion for the esoteric by displaying a unique art book"—
    Provided by publisher.
Identifiers: LCCN 2019029643 (print) | LCCN 2019029644 (ebook) | ISBN
    9780738757247 (trade paperback) | ISBN 9780738757469 (ebook)
Subjects: LCSH: Witchcraft. | Magic.
Classification: LCC BF1571 .H86 2019 (print) | LCC BF1571 (ebook) | DDC
    133.4/3—dc23
LC record available at https://lccn.loc.gov/2019029643
LC ebook record available at https://lccn.loc.gov/2019029644

Llewellyn Publications
A Division of Llewellyn Worldwide Ltd.
2143 Wooddale Drive
Woodbury MN 55125-2989
www.llewellyn.com

Printed in China

SPECIAL LOVE AND DEDICATION

This was no easy book to manifest, and it wouldn't have been possible without my acquisitions editor, Elysia. We planned this book over several years, and she fully supported my vision for it. She was my voice in the meetings, my cheerleader when the process grew laborious, and a constant companion as I tackled the mound of ideas that eventually became the finished product.

The art department at Llewellyn was pretty incredible throughout this whole process as well. I came to them with a really big idea, and they were somehow able to make it happen. I may have taken the photos and drawn a few of the elements, but the rest was up to a team of people who saw the potential in this project.

Jacki Smith, fellow author and owner of Coventry Creations, supplied all but one of the candles you see in this book. When I told her that I was about to go into production on it, she was so excited that she sent me a box of ritual candles from her factory. This is just a tiny piece of the support she has shared with me, and it really made a difference in the quality of the work. She has always been a big fan of *Modern Witch,* and I think it is so cool to have a part of her magic in this book.

The *Modern Witch* community of fans, listeners, readers, and subscribers has been my inspiration throughout this whole process, and I feel blessed to have them in my life. I never knew when I started the podcast and magazine that something so amazing would spring up around it. I love each and every one of you. Thank you for inviting me along on your path and making my work part of your own. Together we will do great things. If you would like to join us, check out ModernWitch.com.

Lastly, I want to send love to my father, Frank, who passed away during the writing of this book. I knew him in life as a supportive, kind, and mystical figure whose interest in the occult and witchcraft was a major inspiration for me early on. His death was a reminder to hold the things that matter close and to see things through to the end, no matter what happens. I love you, Pops.

Contents

INTRODUCTION

We all know there is magic in this universe; things happen that cannot be explained or defined in ways that satiate scientific or critical thinking. Some of us have rationalized the unexplainable and find comfort in knowing that there is an answer for everything. Others know in their gut that there is more than meets the eye and that not everything can be explained rationally. Few, however, actually take the steps to engage the unexplainable and learn on a personal level about the mysteries and power therein. Those people are often known as healers, wizards, warlocks, sorcerers, cunning men, wise women, conjurers, or by one word that seems to fit all of these different labels: witch.

Witchcraft involves the practice of moving beyond merely acknowledging the spiritual nuances that exist in the universe and becoming an active participant in their arrangement.

Witchcraft is a term that describes a diverse set of practices, beliefs, and observances that can be found throughout the world. In some places the craft is seen in the benevolent folk remedies cooked up by faith healers to cure illness, and in other places it is seen as a diabolical tool for corruption that only the most wretched partake of. No matter where you go, however, we witches have always resided on the outskirts of society. We come in all shapes and colors and from every background imaginable. We are your neighbors, your teachers, your doctors, and even the actors you see on television. You may not always see us, but we are always there with our magic.

In truth, the vast majority of witches live as society's outliers. We have been the downtrodden, the forgotten, the lost, the shamed, and the abused. It isn't that witchcraft made us this way, but it usually finds us this way. Regardless of how far we reach back through time, witchcraft has always been a tool for survival for those of us who need it. It gives us the ability to shape and mold life to our own specifications, rather than to force ourselves to acquiesce to the demands of an often cruel and unforgiving world. It is what the poor reach for to find justice, what the desperate turn to for miracles, and where outcasts find security. Witchcraft gives us the ability to live life on our own terms when the odds are stacked against us.

At the core of this ability, regardless of tradition or influence, reside the arts of the five most popular types of magical workings: love, healing, protection, prosperity, and divination. What makes these particular forms of magic so popular is that they happen to affect some of the most important aspects of our lives. Everyone wants to love and be loved. Everyone needs to heal or be healed at some time. Everyone needs to feel safe. Everyone needs help paying the bills and saving money, and everyone needs help navigating the waters of life. With these workings, all of these things become more possible. You don't need to wait for fate; you can create your own.

There is, of course, no such thing as "one spell fits all," so in addition to sharing the techniques and recipes important to performing these arts, we will also discuss ways of adjusting each of them so that they fit your unique needs. What you see here is a collection of spells, recipes, charms, correspondences, and workings that I have collected and used for almost twenty years. These are the magical workings that I have used both for myself and my clients in my career as a professional witch, and now it is time to share them with you.

You will notice that this book is different from other books on magical workings in that there are photos of almost everything we discuss. My first hope is that in providing a visual representation of the workings, you can get a better understanding of what makes each of them successful.

By working magic for
love, healing, protection,
prosperity, and divination, all of
these things become more possible.
You don't need to wait for fate;
you can create your own.

Though it is difficult to capture the essence of magic in photos, each one is a picture of an actual working that was being performed or of something magical. They are images of "live magic," if you will. You will also see scenes from my trips around the country, shots from my living room, and even a few from my backyard.

My other hope is that by seeing these workings and having access to them in this way, you will be inspired to make them yours and try them out in your own life. Sure, you might be able to buy some of these workings from a metaphysical shop or botanica, but there is nothing quite like making magic and learning how to do it for yourself. Blending your own incense and oils that were made for your specific needs gives you a degree of control and connection to your workings that is unparalleled in magic. As we get our hands dirty throughout this book, keep track of the techniques that resonate with you and see where else they might be applied. You may even find that you have a particular knack for certain types of magic.

In closing, we are about to embark on a wild journey together through some of the most sought-after spells, rituals, and workings found in modern witchcraft. Even if this book sits on your coffee table or on a shelf and you only open it once, I hope it helps you connect the dots and build a practice that is wholly your own.

Take what you need from these pages when you need it and always be willing to help out someone else with what you learn. One of the greatest gifts that comes from being a witch is the ability to help others when they need it.

Chapter 1

FIRST STEPS

Witchcraft can be useful in just about any situation in life and can help us to bring big change when needed. While there are some really deep and fascinating aspects of occultism and mysticism that can be quite useful to study, there are five things that you should always keep in mind when approaching the craft. These are the essential philosophies that, when applied, help you to cast the most effective spells possible and also create the magical life required for long-term manifestation.

We live in a universe that is composed entirely of energy, and you must use that to your advantage. The phrase "mind over matter" suggests that thought can shape the physical world. Since the universe is composed of energy, then that must mean the mind and matter are made of the same stuff. In theory, this also means that all things are connected, even the unknown, in a similar manner. The mind is much more than just thought, however; it is also part of your soul, and it houses personality, subjective reality, and motivation. Wise witches know to give over all of the energy when casting a spell or else they will remain personally tied to its outcome. This means that while you are performing magic, you must be present in mind, body, and soul, and you must disconnect from all work once it is completed. In addition, you have to be wholly convinced that the spell will be successful. Otherwise, you run the risk of the influence from the working affecting you in a sort of feedback loop or of it falling flat upon takeoff.

When we perform works for others or on others, it is imperative that we let it all go before finishing the working. For instance, if you were casting a banishing spell, you would want to be entirely done with what you are banishing or else the spell just won't work because you would continue to be connected. Likewise, when you cast a spell for money, you can't finish the spell and still be frantically concerned about money. It may take some time, but always remember that doubt is the most significant block to making this happen. In addition, perform cleansing work on yourself regularly (as described in this chapter) to keep your energy clear of blocks and lingering effects.

Energy is flowing everywhere around you, and it follows the path of least resistance. This means that having a magical influence on a situation or environment requires a path to exist in the first place. This is one of the reasons why we work with a set of what are called correspondences. Essentially, a correspondence is an object or existing archetype that carries a similar energy signature to what we are trying to achieve. Certain herbs, stones, spirits, etc., will correspond to a required energy, and because of this, we can work with them as agents of magic.

This also means that you must be sure to be free of resistance to your own magic. For example, you can't cast a spell to get a job and never turn in any applications. You can't do a spell for better overall health and expect it to work if you are eating fried food every night. Magic can only work with what it is given in the first place. In addition to performing cleansings, you must be sure to look for where resistance might rest and include that in your magical thinking. Sometimes simple changes can remove significant blocks toward manifestation.

Silence is golden. Once you cast a spell or perform a working, keep your mouth shut and tell no one until it is complete. Until a spell has come to fruition, it is still able to be influenced by others. If you tell someone you did a spell for success, for example, their own desire for success or what they think success should look like for you could get in the way. Furthermore, if you did a working and are talking about it before it is done, you are reconnecting with it, which essentially creates resistance.

Witchcraft is an art form as well as a spiritual path. There really is no wrong way to practice the craft, so you might as well let yourself have some fun. Sure, I am giving you a few things to live by, but ultimately the choices are up to you. Once you get the swing of things and understand the concepts behind spell work, you are able to take matters into your own hands and create your own magic. I think this is an essential step for all witches—to leave the books behind and simply create for the sake of creating.

When you perform an act of bewitchment, let yourself be an artist and create something beautiful, no matter the working. Magic is often

> **⋮**
>
> *Witchcraft is an art
> form as well as a spiritual
> path. There really is no wrong
> way to practice the craft, so you
> might as well let yourself
> have some fun.*

just as much about weaving together correspondences that express the energy required for the working as it is about doing so in a manner that incorporates visual elements. We often work magic in what is known as "sympathetic" style, which means that we incorporate elements symbolically associated with an event or person, such as using an herb that resembles a part of the body in a healing spell because it resembles the desired organ, sticking a pin through a doll to affect a region of the body, or braiding cords to bring multiple elements of magic together. We also work with certain colors and scents because they represent or have a connection to a desired influence—and while it's not quite the same thing as sympathetic magic, it follows the same line of thinking. Wherever there is magic, there are visual elements that help drive the working.

Magic will help create the life you want. Keeping all four of the first principles in mind, understand that if you are able to live life in a way where witchcraft becomes an integral part of it, your witchcraft will be stronger and, as a result, the influence you are able to have will become stronger. I often think of the craft as a "spiritual lifestyle." Keep an altar where you can perform magic, even if it is a simple one, and visit it regularly to keep your mind on magic. When you visit a new place, reach out with your senses and try to feel the different types of energy that surround you. When you shower, do so with the thought that water is purifying your energy body as well as your physical body. Include magic in your approach to new beginnings or endings, to the things that worry you, and in the fight to live a better life.

———————

Remember these principles as you move through this book so that you can truly get the most out of your experience. In the bibliography there is a list of amazing books on the craft that I turn to when I need inspiration and clarity. Check out those books and resources if you feel like exploring further!

Magic will help create
the life you want

ETHICS

One of the topics that the witchcraft community struggles with in the modern age is the place where witchcraft and ethics intersect. After hundreds of years of being feared, and of that fear turning into danger, many witches began to adopt a "harm none" policy starting around the 1960s. This led to a bit of a white-washing of witchcraft, but in many ways it became a sort of armor for witches around the world when the Satanic Panic of the 1980s took over. At that time witchcraft and mysticism were coming out of the closet in some really big ways, and we witnessed a resurgence of interest in the old ways. Had it not been for many witches adopting and publicly speaking about their belief in harming none, there likely would have been much more pressure on witches in the modern day.

Not all witches have adopted "harm none."
It isn't a rule that has to be followed or an
absolute of any kind; it is a spiritual principle
you adopt, similar to being a pacifist.

While most of us do not enjoy becoming violent, we do believe in protecting ourselves. This is mostly the case with witches and cursing. We don't want to curse—we will always try to do everything to avoid it—but if we perceive a threat great enough, we would. This is something that is entirely up to you.

I believe that ethics are relative to a situation. As I will discuss throughout this book, witchcraft is, in many ways, a spiritual approach to a life where the odds are stacked against you. Some of us come to the craft for empowerment; some feel drawn to the spiritual aesthetic. Many people also turn to the craft to get justice when it isn't being served, to protect their families when no one is there to protect them, or to find help when everything feels insurmountable. Very few people have turned to the craft as a first resort; generally, it is the very last thing they try before losing all hope. Who are we to judge or demand that those who are suffering play nice?

Living by a set of values and standards is more important than living by a code of ethics. As a witch, you will come face to face with many challenges. Ethics might fail you, your highest ideals might fail you, even your confidence might fail you. Life doesn't always afford us such comforts. If, however, you live with a set of standards, you will always have something to strive for. We should set a standard of being good people both in and outside of the magical world. But I believe we should also have the standard of living a safe and healthy life. When that is not possible, there is plenty of magic out there to help solve that problem. While we won't get into cursing in this book, I advise you to keep an open mind when you come across the material. If anything, understanding how it is done will assist you if you ever need to protect yourself or someone else from a curse. Whether or not you choose to partake in them, the only rules against them are the ones that you agree too. A word of advice, however: what you generate, you will attract.

WHERE TO PRACTICE AND EXPLORE MAGIC

Magic and the opportunity to interact with it is all around us. I find that spending time in nature, away from the hustle and bustle of everyday life in the suburbs or city, is the best way to feel it. We cannot always get out and make magic in the wilderness, however, so what is a witch to do? We find ways of bringing aspects of the magical into our lives, regardless of where we may be. This isn't always easy, but if we were to have one magical space or place to visit, it should be an altar.

Altars act as stations of magic and power. Once they are built and consecrated, they become conduits for spiritual energy that will constantly remain active unless disempowered. An altar can be any shape or size, hidden or visible, private or public; it doesn't matter. What matters, however, is that it be respected as a sacred space. In addition to being a place of power, an altar is the meeting point for you and the spirits you will be working with.

*Witch power is responsible
for your interest in magic, your
connection to the unseen worlds, and
your psychic abilities. Exploring and
understanding the pieces of you that
create your own **unique** witch
power will help you to become
a force of nature.*

SETTING UP AN ALTAR

All you really need for an altar is a flat surface, and even that is negotiable. The altar will be where you go to perform your magic, but it doesn't even necessarily need to be stationary. For many years I kept all of my altar supplies in a wooden box that I could take with me wherever I needed to go. This gave me the ability to hide my supplies when I needed to and transport them easily. Nowadays I have altars all over my home and even in my car.

Your altar can have as many items as you need on it, and the more you do magic there, the stronger the altar's overall resonance will become.

For the purposes of spells and workings of a more general sort, the altar only needs to be a space used for magic. If you practice witchcraft religiously, your altar is likely to be a place of worship and devotion, with a stricter set of requirements.

Physically clean the space that is to be your altar so that you start with a fresh surface. Before you put anything on it, bless and consecrate it as your altar. To do this, place your hands six inches or so above the surface and close your eyes. Take a few deep breaths; once you feel grounded and focused, place your hands on the altar and say:

> *By magic right I claim this space;*
> *Here be power and thus its place!*
> *Upon this altar I part the veil;*
> *With the witch power I now set sail!*
> *As I command it, so must this be.*
> *For the good of all, but mostly for me!*

By magic right
I claim this space

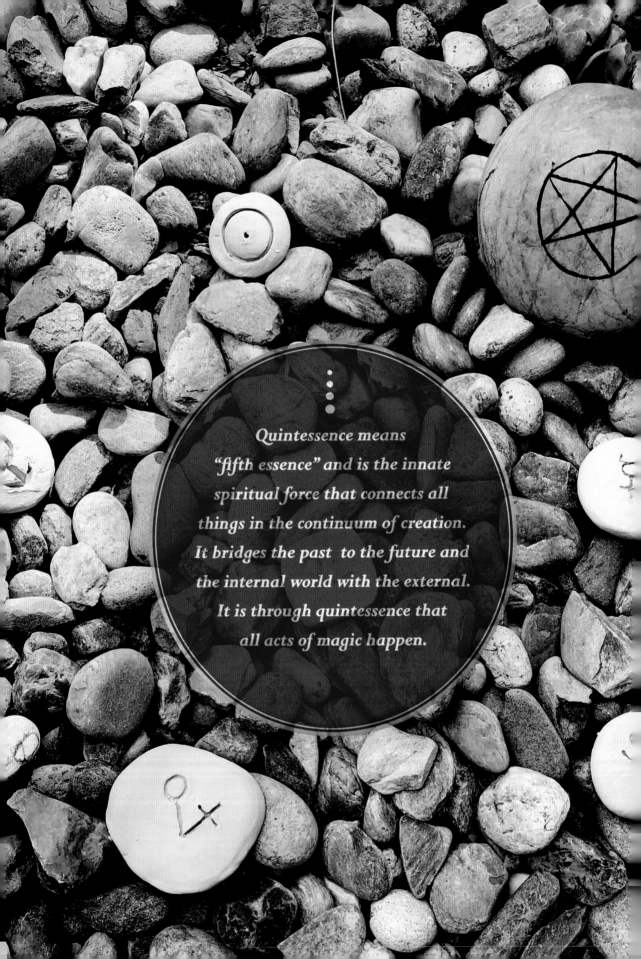

Quintessence means
"fifth essence" and is the innate
spiritual force that connects all
things in the continuum of creation.
It bridges the past to the future and
the internal world with the external.
It is through quintessence that
all acts of magic happen.

On your altar place things that embody the type of work you want to do, such as crystals, talismans, and your preferred divination tools. If you are working with a certain spirit or deity, have a statue or picture of them as well as a place to make offerings. Most importantly, have a candle on the altar that symbolizes your connection to quintessence and the witch power. As we move through this book, we will look at different ways of working with candles, but for now, all this needs to be is a candle of any color or size that you can light during times of meditation and focus. This isn't a candle to use in spells or other workings, but one that is only lit when you are actively reaching out to connect with the powers and influences around you. Think of it as a signal to the magical aspects of the universe that you are open and ready for business.

PREPARING FOR A WORKING

Keeping in mind that energy follows the path of least resistance, our first steps toward creating bewitchment of any kind come in the form of preparation. There are a handful of preparatory acts that we should do before we move on to performing a working. These will help us to remove obstacles that might otherwise get in the way.

———————

Research. The first thing to do is research your working. Know not just who or what you are performing the working on, but why you are doing the working and what you want to happen. Magic doesn't always work out the way you want it to; however, most of the time this can be corrected by doing a little research and planning beforehand. For example, if you were to cast a spell for a specific resolution in a court case, you would want to make sure you knew what the case entailed and, based on this information, what the optimal outcome could be. If you cast a spell to attract a new partner but aren't specific about what you are looking for and how you want that partner to fit into your life, there are any number of possible suitors who could come knocking.

Another thing to consider is what you might have to do mundanely as part of the spell to allow it to happen, such as sending out a résumé after a job spell, going to a meeting over an issue you're working magic on, going to a doctor in conjunction with your healing work if you are ill, etc. If you can get all the details and pinpoint your specific needs and desires before entering a spell or ritual, that working often will be much more efficient. The final thing to consider is to perform an act of divination to get more insight. We will go over methods for this in the divination chapter, but it is worth mentioning here.

Gather supplies. Next, make sure you have everything you need to do the working. This means that you need to see what ingredients or items you have and what you will need to grab. This doesn't always mean you need to go out and buy expensive herbs or tools to make things work; sometimes it just means seeing how you can make what you already have work for your needs. Often there is a perfectly natural and free alternative to an item that can be found in nature or in everyday life. Whatever you work with or choose to use in your magic, during preparation it is time to collect these things and have them ready for the working. You don't want to start a spell and then have to stop halfway through because you forgot something. Sure, you can stop and jump back in, but often this gums up the works.

Align and ground your energy. The easiest method for this is to focus on taking slow, steady, deep breaths for a few minutes and meditate on the concept of releasing any mental or physical tension that is keeping you from being present and in the moment. One way to do this is by envisioning yourself growing roots from your feet that travel deep into the earth beneath you. As you breathe, allow your energy to harmonize with that of the ground, releasing excess energy and replenishing needed stores.

You can also chant the mantra "I am now, I am earth; I am magic, I am worth!" as you visualize these roots taking hold and restoring equilibrium with the earth.

One of my preferred methods of aligning and grounding my energy is to perform a mind/body/spirit invocation. This is a method I developed that infuses multiple techniques to get the job done and bring all of my parts together to be in the moment. This keeps our mind from wandering, allows our bodies to feel the magic we are performing, and lets us be guided by our highest good. You can't really go wrong there, and all you need is a place free of distraction.

THE MIND/BODY/SPIRIT INVOCATION

Breathe slow and deep, focusing on the points of stillness and silence at the beginning and end of each breath. As you do this, check in with yourself. Have you been upset or overwhelmed? Are you happy or sad? Take a moment and really ask yourself how you are doing. If there isn't anything you can do about it at the moment, release that thought and allow yourself to move on for now. All we need to focus on is the now. Next, check in with your physical body. How does it feel? Are you comfortable? Sore? Again, if there is nothing you can do about it at the moment, simply acknowledge it and move on. Lastly, check in with your spirit. Do you feel connected and tuned in to the spiritual energies around you? Do you feel your spirit guides and ancestors? Do you feel a sense of purpose? Take another moment, acknowledge, and move on.

Take another deep breath and focus on your mind again. Say:

> *I draw my focus to the mind, keeper of all that I know,*
> *and open it like a flower to this moment.*
> *I call upon the powers within to bring clarity and wisdom!*

Bring your awareness to your body and say:

> *I draw my focus to the body, temple of flesh and bone,*
> *and feel my strength at this moment.*
> *I call upon the powers within to bring potency and action!*

Take another deep breath and bring your attention to your spirit. Say:

I draw my focus to the spirit, a spark of the divine,
and find purpose at this moment.
I call upon the powers within to bring inspiration and ecstasy!

Lastly, take one final breath and say:

Mind, body, and spirit are one; at this moment it is done!

Salt of the earth
water of life
Cleanse this space
of illness and strife

Smudge to spiritually cleanse yourself, your tools, and your space.
The most common methods for doing this are burning sage (smudging)
or cleansing by salt (known as an "earth cleansing").

Truthfully, you can smudge with any cleansing herb that isn't toxic;
sage just happens to be the preferred herb, and it has a long history of
serving us in this way. Some people do experience negative side effects
from burning sage, as it can release a chemical that elevates depression
and anxiety in rare cases. It also may not be possible for you to burn
sage in your apartment or dorm. You can make a liquid smudge spray by
adding 10 drops of sage essential oil to 4 ounces distilled or spring water
in a spray bottle. This is an excellent way to still work with sage without
needing to worry about burning it.

An earth cleansing is done by working with salt. You can make a saltwater solution by mixing roughly 1 tablespoon of sea salt with 1 cup of
room-temperature water. Once the salt dissolves, it can be added to a
spray bottle or you can dip your fingers into it and then flick droplets
around the desired area or person. As you do this, say, "Salt of the earth,
water of life, cleanse this space of illness and strife!"

*You can also work with salt directly by
rubbing some on the bottom of your feet
and the palms of your hands while you
visualize it scrubbing away negative energy
and reestablishing your earth connection.*

For both the sage and salt methods, you will need to introduce the
cleansing agent to an area where you will be performing magic. You will
want to run your tools through the sage smoke or gently flick/spray the
enhanced water on them. To cleanse yourself, do the same as you did

for your tools, and allow the smoke to waft over and around all limbs, your neck, and your torso. If you are using the saltwater method, dip your fingers in the water and dab your forehead, heart, palms, navel, and feet, each time dipping back into the water and visualizing a white light emerging from the places you touch and working its way outward to cover your entire body.

Keep these things in mind before performing a working and do everything you can to remove obstacles that could get between you and the manifestation of your magic.

Let's be real: no one wants to go through all the trouble of casting a spell or adjusting their vibration just to have it all go flat because they didn't prepare themselves for a working. A lot of magical calamities can be avoided simply by preparing ourselves.

When in doubt, take a ritual bath or shower! It is possible that I am a little biased—if I could spend my day in the shower, I probably would—but one of my favorite ways to keep myself spiritually cleansed is to perform some form of ritual bathing daily.

Like all things in witchcraft, there are many ways to do this, but in general all the necessary ingredients are easily found. To a warm bath, add a cup of sea salt and your favorite herbs and essential oils. As long as the salt is there, any herb or flower should help to raise your vibration. In general, I find that adding fresh rose petals, hyssop, and lemongrass can give an excellent boost. If you don't have a bathtub, your shower will do just fine! In a large bowl, mix your salt and other ingredients with warm water and then pour the mixture over your head. Contain the herby bits in a cheesecloth or muslin bag so they don't clog your drains.

Add a cup of sea salt
and your favorite herbs
and essential oils to
a warm bath

BLESSING AND CHARGING
THINGS FOR MAGIC

Sometime before or during your working, you will likely want to bless and charge an item with the intention of it being used in magic. Blessing and charging are similar but have two separate intentions. Blessings are always positive. Any good energy you send is technically a blessing. The opposite of a blessing is a curse, which is a totally different book and is seen as a complete magical act all unto itself. For example, we bless our food before eating it, or we bless a child with good luck before sending them off to school. Charging an item, on the other hand, is like a blessing, but the item being charged will be worked with as an active agent in your magic. We charge candles with intention and willpower before lighting them. We charge a stone to carry a specific vibration. These aren't singular acts of magic, like a blessing, but rather a step among several in a magical process.

Believe it or not, the easiest way to bless something is by blowing it a kiss or actually kissing it and saying a little prayer. It makes sense; we kiss our lovers and our children, both forms of love and goodwill, just shaped differently for the receiver. I am the weird bearded guy driving down the highway and blowing kisses at the cars stopped along the sides of the road, praying that their day gets easier. It never hurts to send a little blessing to someone who is having a difficult time.

Charging an item is easy and should be done whenever possible. It helps to clarify your intention and bring focus to your working. Ideally, every item used in your magic should be charged before use. This gets a little tedious and I know many witches who just skip this altogether, but there is immense benefit in going about things in this manner.

A happy medium, which I prefer, is to wait until I have constructed any elements needed for the working and then charge them before use. That means that if I need to carve a candle or dress it with herbs and oils, I wait until I have done so before charging anything, otherwise I would need to charge the oil, candle, and herbs separately. Like I said, it can get tedious. By getting all the work out of the way, we can remain more focused on the other parts of the magic when it is time.

The easiest way
to bless something
is by blowing it
a kiss and saying
a little prayer.

To charge something, I draw a pentacle in the air over or in front of it with my index and middle fingers. As I do this, I also perform two important tasks. The first is that I visualize the pentacle being drawn with a liquid blue flame that hovers in the air where my fingers have been. The second is that while doing all of this, I command (not ask, command) the object to be the representative of all the correspondences and energy gathered there, as well as any energy connected to those correspondences, as a singular force where all parts are working together.

It usually goes something like:

> *It is my will that this (insert name of item here) be the*
> *perfect representation of my focus and magic on this plane.*
> *May all its parts work in tandem, and may it bring about*
> *the change I seek!*

You should make it as personal as you need to. Once the pentacle has been drawn and programmed, push the pentacle into the object you are charging with your hands. As you do this, visualize the pentacle getting smaller and smaller until it is absorbed into the object.

WHAT TO DO DURING A WORKING

Performing a magical working can take anywhere from five seconds to five years, all depending on the method. Sometimes they are done in one sitting; some are done over a series of sittings. The important things are to not rush yourself or your magic and to remain present when you are actively performing any working. Much can be lost by allowing the mind to drift away and lose focus. Much can also be gained by truly being in the moment and allowing all of your senses to engage the quintessence that swirls around and through you.

If you are fully present in your working, it will tell you what it needs to be successful. What I mean by this is that your instincts, led by your intuition, will inform you as to exactly what you need to do. This requires you to listen to your gut and speak from the heart. If you find yourself overwhelmed by an emotion, pay attention to that emotion and ask yourself how it serves you and the working. Then allow that emotion to become part of the working and the energy used to make it happen. If you find yourself with the urge to light more incense than is instructed, go for it.

If you find yourself not feeling it in the middle of the spell, then slow down and ask your senses what is needed in the moment. As my first teacher would say, "Listening to your gut is the best way to ensure success!"

Be respectful of the working and of any spirits who are present. Use your senses to feel for the presence of allies in your workings, then ask them for advice and help when needed. The law of animism says that there is an indwelling spirit in all things, which means there is a spirit associated with every ingredient and tool that you include in your workings. When in doubt, reach out to these beings for advice and clarity. To do this, you merely need to be present in mind, body, and spirit. Focus on the spiritual presence of the item and then pose it a question in your mind. Take a deep breath and allow the response to come to you in the same way inspiration might come to you. The first response is always the correct response.

WHAT TO DO AFTER A WORKING

In addition to doing a possible cleansing on yourself and the working space, you will need a plan of action regarding how you take care of your spell remnants. When all is said and done, the candle will burn out, the herbs will turn to ashes, and the poppet will need a place to live.

My general rule is that if you don't want to hold on to the energy, throw it away or recycle it. If you do want to hold on to it, either bury it or keep it somewhere safe, where no one else will have access to it.

Have faith and wait patiently for things to begin happening. Be open to the powers you work with communicating with you through synchronicity, dreams, and divination. When you get a sign or receive information about your bewitchment, document it. When you find that it has worked—or perhaps didn't work—document that result as well. All of this will be useful when you cast the spell again in the future or base other methods off of the success or failure of the documented method. Witchcraft can often include trial and error at times, and that is okay.

Have faith and wait patiently

Chapter 2
THE STUFF MAGIC IS MADE OF

Witchcraft is the art of weaving various energies together to create a magical influence. We don't just start adding things to the cauldron willy-nilly, however. Every item and piece of information used to create our magic has a specific purpose and intention. As I mentioned earlier, a correspondence is an object or existing archetype that carries a similar energy signature to what we are trying to achieve. Certain herbs, stones, spirits, etc., will correspond to a required energy, and because of this we can work with them as agents of magic. For instance, we work with specific herbs to attract money, certain gemstones to help us heal, and particular symbols to help us connect to hidden forces. There are many different types of correspondences out there, and every vein of magical practice is likely to have their own set of them. Think of correspondences as a component of the magic you are performing, or as ingredients. Each correspondence lends a special something that makes the entire working manifest.

Let's take a look at the most common correspondences and how they are used in witchcraft.

WORKING WITH THE MINERAL KINGDOM
in Magic

The mineral kingdom includes all matter that is a natural-forming compound and is usually inorganic. This includes metals, elemental deposits, and minerals like common, semiprecious, and precious gemstones. This kingdom is intrinsically tied to humankind. Some minerals—such as calcium, magnesium, zinc, and iron—are so vital to the human body that to be low in them could lead to frailty or fatality. Gem and semiprecious stones have been prized and coveted since the dawn of civilization for their beauty as well as their obvious power, each stone having been studied and profiled for its magical and spiritual qualities. Metal has had an even more significant impact, leading to advanced machinery and weaponry, industrial revolutions, and the advancement of civilization. Many witches believe that the start of the Bronze Age also coincided with a great separation between humans and the beings of spirit and magic that once ruled alongside us.

We work with minerals in magic primarily as supplemental energy for our own energy body in the same way that we use vitamins as supplements for the physical body. They can help us by doing everything from protecting us and strengthening our aura to assisting in the healing process and elevating the mood in an entire home.

Working with Gemstones

The words "crystal" and "gemstone" are often used interchangeably in metaphysics, but technically they are two different things. A crystal is a substance that is both pure and contains a repeating ordered arrangement of atoms. There are a lot of minerals that are crystalline in structure, but not all crystals are gemstones. Salt is a crystal mineral, for example.

Gemstones are minerals that are prized and valued for three reasons: rarity, durability, and attractiveness. They usually form in the earth, and once mined they are polished and sometimes cut to resemble crystalline structures. Gemstone quality depends on clarity and color depth, with an emphasis on its rarity. Some minerals that have organic origins, such as amber, jet, coral, and petrified wood, are still considered to be gemstones.

Gemstones can be both expensive and hard to find if you aren't living close to a store that sells them. Don't worry if you cannot find the specific stone listed or if you don't have one of the stones listed as a substitute in each chapter. We will be working with stones in many different ways throughout this book, and you should feel invited to come up with your own approaches to incorporating crystals into your magic.

Here is a list of stones I think every witch should have:

Clear quartz for general witchcraft, mental and spiritual clarity, and to store energy. Whenever you're in a pinch, always remember that clear quartz can do the job of just about any stone. In fact, if you were going to buy just one stone and wanted the most versatile one possible, clear quartz is it! It is quickly cleansed and programmed and—most importantly—easy to come by. Clear quartz also seems to have an affinity for working with humans, so it is one of the easiest stones to work with, especially when a practitioner is new to stones.

Black tourmaline for energy, protection, and to help during the healing process. This stone makes for one heck of a grounding stone that will help the energy body release excess energy. Black tourmaline is also known for its ability to pierce through deception and guide witches to the hidden truth. For this reason, it is also prized as an all-around protection stone.

Citrine for clarity, wealth, and cleansing. Citrine is one of a handful of stones that requires no cleansing; it is often used to assist in the energetic cleansing of other stones and spaces. It is known as a "commerce stone" and has a long history of being placed in cash boxes to draw money and as an altar stone to aid in the accumulation of wealth. It is known to assist in debt banishment and is reported to assist in the healing process for those with viral and bacterial infections.

Rose quartz for self-love, empathy, and to attract general positive vibrations. This stone is very popular because of its pink hue and ability to help with the emotional healing process. It helps to establish connections with others and has a sweetening effect on people who harbor ill feelings toward you. This stone is also popular for its ability to protect from mental abuse.

Amethyst for psychic sensitivity, help with addictions and bad habits, and to help keep the mind sharp when performing magic. This is a stone that was once prized by pirates for its ability to help sober them up. It is a stone highly related to the energies of the Goddess and the powers of intuition and psychicism, and it is often worn by witches to help increase sensitivity. Amethyst will also assist in dreamwork and in the banishing of nightmares.

Lapis lazuli for psychic power, protection, prosperity, and connecting with divine forces. This stone has been prized as a magical stone by cultures all over the world, most notably the ancient Egyptians. It is said that wearing lapis lazuli will bring good luck and protection from evil spirits. Lapis is known for helping those who are developing their psychic ability to do so with ease, and it is often worked with to aid witches during acts of conjuration. Most notably, lapis can help make contact with powerful spirits, such as the gods.

Selenite for clearing the aura and energy body, assisting in contact with the higher self, and for work related to exorcism. Selenite contains a lot of calcium and is known for its ability to catch the light and throw it like a moonbeam. You can use selenite in place of a sage smudge as it will help to filter and purify your energy body in the same way. Placed at the entryways of the home, selenite will assist in the overall communication and emotional connection of the household. Inexpensive in comparison to most stones, this stone can also be used to banish or exorcise hard-to-budge energies.

Use clear quartz for general witchcraft and to store energy

Most stones come from the earth and in some cases took millions of years to form. Even a tiny piece can connect you with that energy. Wear them in jewelry or keep them in your pocket to drape their energy around you like a cloak. Keep a piece on your desk to aid the mind. Place a piece at the front door to attract the energy it represents, or set a stone on the altar to bring focus to your workings.

When it comes to crystals and minerals, there are few rules. Some stones, however, are known to be toxic if worked with in rough forms, such as malachite, which can cause major complications in pregnancy, or bumblebee jasper (also known as eclipse stone), which contains both arsenic and sulfur. Research each stone before you work with it to make sure you are using it wisely.

Working with Metals

Metals are a bit different as they are technically minerals that can conduct both electricity and heat. Because of this, metals make excellent aids in magic. The list of available metals to work with ranges from iron and tin to zinc and gold. Not all metals are easily obtained or safe to work with, however. Lead and mercury are dangerous to handle; though they have a history of being worked with in magic, they are best avoided now that we know better.

In magic there are metals that we often work with and are nontoxic to handle:

Gold is prized as being connected to the sun and is associated with wealth, abundance, healing, and the highest spiritual vibrations. It can assist in bringing balance to a location or situation, and it assists in the decision-making process. Gold is also worked with for purity, stabilization, and rejuvenation. It is the metal of the divine masculine.

Silver is seen as being connected to the moon and is associated with intuition, empathy, psychic abilities, and dreams. It can be used in spiritual work related to the soul and its health, as well as to connect to the nurturing influences of the universe. Silver is also worked with to eliminate obstacles and strengthen the properties of gemstones. It is the metal of the divine feminine.

Copper is connected to Venus and associated with balance, nutrition, love, and connection between the worlds. It assists in the harmonization of the physical and spiritual worlds and is said to aid in the manifestation of one's magic. Copper is also worked with to heal the mind-body connection and to assist in all manner of communication.

Bronze is a mix of copper and around 12 percent tin. It is used in faery magic and workings related to ancestors or the mighty dead.

Brass is a mix of copper and 30 percent or more of zinc. It is used in magic to communicate with ascended masters and angels.

Iron is perhaps worked with the most in witchcraft as it has properties that can be used to both strengthen and nullify magic. As a strengthener, iron can be added in protection magic of any kind as well as workings related to healing the blood or cooling the temper. Used to separate etheric patterns, iron can be worked with much like salt but to greater effect. Iron is used to prevent magical attacks and to stop psychic energy from amassing. It is also used effectively in the total grounding of energy when necessary.

Witches should keep a piece of iron on their altars at all times, both for protection and to keep mischief from spirits such as faeries from wreaking havoc on their magic.

Magic is never out
of reach and can be found
anytime we need it. Literally
anything can be used in magic.
Have faith, look it up, and
be creative with what is
already around you.

Plants are food and medicine, but they also carry magical properties in addition to their potential medicinal properties.

WORKING WITH THE PLANT KINGDOM
in Magic

We work with herbs and trees for several reasons, and it is assumed that long before witches were working with stones and crystals, we were working with the plant kingdom. Plants are food and medicine, but they also carry magical properties in addition to their potential medicinal properties.

Plants are used in the craft to help do everything from cleanse and empower to exorcize, and I have never met a witch who didn't have an affinity for one herb or another.

Some herbs can be toxic or cause an allergic reaction, so do a little research before working with them. Just because something comes from nature doesn't make it safe to consume. Make wise choices.

In this book we will take a look at different ways of working with the plant kingdom in magic, mostly the making of incense and oils. We make incense to combine, focus, and release the energy within the herbs and resins. We blend oils to wear and to dress our candles and other magical tools. Each of these applications works with the plant's energy in a different way and helps to release it into a working for a specific purpose.

Working with the plant kingdom to make incense is a common and versatile technique. We all have our favorite stick incense that we can find at the corner store, but making incense for magic is an amazing way to work with the plant kingdom. For the most part, all we need to do is grind our ingredients together and burn them over charcoal or add a little something extra to make them self-lighting. I use an old coffee bean grinder to grind all my herbs, but you can always go old-school and use a mortar and pestle. When making incense, it is usually preferable to powder each ingredient or risk having an uneven burn.

Combusting your incense is easy, but you need to use precautions. Only burn a small amount at a time. Always use a burner or a firesafe dish with sand or salt to catch falling ash and debris, and always make sure there is good air circulation. The charcoal used most often for burning incense is actually made for use in hookahs and is sold in smoke shops and metaphysical stores. Use a pair of tongs to keep yourself from getting burned, and always avoid directly handling a lit coal. You should also avoid using charcoal that is made for grilling.

To make an incense self-lighting, add an equal amount of makko powder to the mix. You can add a small amount of water to make a thick, clay-like paste from which you form cones that you then dry to make your own cone incense.

While there are tons of herbs that deserve love and appreciation, this is a list of the herbs I think every witch should try to have in their arsenal:

Sage for cleansing and general maintenance. As we discussed earlier in this chapter, sage is super useful when it comes to ridding ourselves of unwanted energy. Burn it when smudging, or make a tea and add the water to your baths and floor washes.

Rue for magic and protection from harm. Classically associated with the Goddess of witchcraft, rue is a formidable magical ally that loves to be used in magic. It can help aid the connection of the mind, body, and spirit as well as when channeling power or energy from a secondary source. It is also a fierce protector and can be carried or placed on the altar to keep you safe from spiritual attack.

Calendula for prosperity and bewitchment. Calendula is known for its ability to bring out the truth in a matter, assist in the growth of prosperity, and aid witches who are attempting to gain influence over a person or situation. Add some to your bath before a working to bring out your inner strength, keep a piece of the flower in your shoe when you go to a job interview for the first time, or drink tea with calendula to aid in public speaking or contract brokering with spirits.

Dragon's blood for potent magic and swift results. Dragon's blood is a resin that comes from the dracaena tree that is native to India and Australia. The sap of the tree bleeds red when cut and is harvested and dried to produce the resin. It will assist any act of magic, where it is known for having a neutral masculine/feminine energy charge and is prized for its ability to bring all the components of a working together.

Lavender for luck in love and psychic clarity. A cousin to sage, I like to keep lavender handy as it has many uses. Add it to a bath for a calming effect after work or before ritual. Place it in an eye pillow to bring peaceful dreams. Use it in incense to open psychic pathways, or put a piece of it in your pocket before meeting a potential partner for the first time.

Oak for personal strength and spiritual wisdom. Prized for their massive size, oak trees are sacred to the God of witchcraft as well as to seers and those who feel weak or lost. Oak makes an excellent wand. When burned, oak stabilizes the powers of ritual and magic, and it is said to bring focus to all worlds. Making charms and talismans from oak wood or acorns is said to bring strength to our workings.

Bay for secrecy and vision. Bay leaves can be burned to bring about protection from prying eyes and to keep your workings hidden from others. Bay can also be brewed into a tea for psychic vision and protection that can be drunk before performing divination. If you feel you are under magical attack, take a bath with bay leaves and lemon peel to sever connections.

Powder each ingredient
when making incense

Essential, Fragrance, and Condition Oils

Another great way to work with a plant and its spirit is to incorporate essential oils into your magic. Essential oils are naturally occurring oils extracted from plant material, and most can be used both therapeutically and spiritually. In general, we try to avoid direct contact with the skin, so applying essential oils directly to the skin is best done with a carrier oil such as fractionated coconut or sweet almond. When the essential oil is added to these mostly scentless carrier oils, the essential oil is diluted enough so it can be applied to the skin.

Fragrance oils are laboratory produced, contain no plant material, and are used specifically to introduce a fragrance. This can be handy with certain essential oils such as dragon's blood or oakmoss absolute, which are expensive and hard to come by. Fragrance oils are usually easy to find and are used to make magical products that require a heavy or long-lasting scent. Magically speaking, the only boon we can get from working with this type of oil comes from its aroma.

Condition oils are ritually blended to create a magical influence. Scent isn't necessarily a factor, as these oils are blended with magical intent in mind rather than creating a pleasing fragrance.

Both essential and fragrance oils can be used in the creation of a condition oil, as well as other ingredients such as herbs, crystals, curios, etc. In the following chapters there are multiple condition oil recipes in addition to lists of essential oils corresponding to the subject. Feel free to mix them up or exchange one ingredient for another when appropriate and necessary. The tradition of condition oils is often linked to spiritual workers for hire, so it is likely that your local metaphysical shop carries premade condition oils. Condition oils can be added to poppets, charm bags, and fetishes, and they can also be applied directly to petition papers, amulets, statues, talismans, and minerals as an act of blessing or consecration.

We will be working with essential and condition oils in this book. I tend to avoid fragrance oils when possible as they can have a chemical smell. There is, however, a long history of witches and folk magic practitioners using fragrance oils and even extracts in condition oils. Again, feel free to experiment and use what you have!

While all essential oils have a spiritual resonance, there are a few that stick out to me as being important to have on hand if possible:

White sage for exorcism, space clearing, and to increase general activity. Add 10 drops of white sage oil to a 4-ounce spray bottle. Fill with distilled water and then shake vigorously to make a liquid smudge.

Lavender for luck, love, and psychic awareness. Add 7 drops of lavender essential oil to 1 tablespoon of fractionated coconut oil and rub on the bottoms of your feet before bed to have prophetic dreams.

Lemongrass for prosperity and a positive outlook. Diffuse lemongrass essential oil in the morning to help wake you up and create a positive mood to start your day.

Patchouli for sex, money, and the divine masculine. Patchouli essential oil comes in a few varieties; my favorite is dark patchouli, which has a deeper scent. Add 3 drops of patchouli essential oil to a full bath before a date to ensure a good time.

Rose for love, empowerment, and the divine feminine. Rose essential oil shows up in a lot of blends—it is known for providing a floral or green undertone to mixes—but be careful: rose essential oil is also known for taking over blends, so a little goes a long way. Diffuse rose essential oil before ritual to call the powers of the Goddess to you.

Hyssop for breaking curses and bad luck, raising the vibration of a working, or for an all-around blessing. Add 10 drops hyssop essential oil to a 4-ounce spray bottle, fill with distilled water, and then shake well to create an after-ritual self-care spray to help restore energy levels.

Frankincense for magic, consecration, and cleansing. Frankincense essential oil can be added to just about any oil and be complementary due to its earthy and citrus tones, so the fact that it is known to bring focus to spiritual energies makes this one versatile oil to work with in magic. Diffuse in your ritual space before, during, or after to bring balance and clarity to the energies present.

WORKING WITH COSMIC FORCES
in Magic

Astrology has become a bit of a lost art in witchcraft, but it remains a cornerstone in understanding the influences that we and our magic will fall under. Essentially, astrology is the study of the movements of celestial bodies and how they influence the affairs of humanity and the natural world. Just about everyone is familiar with their horoscope, but astrology can be used for so much more. Many witches get overwhelmed by it or take it a bit too seriously and find it restrictive in their workings. In my magic, astrology helps me to develop the best approach more than being something that I absolutely must live by. It can get complicated, but only if you let it! For me, astrology is a way to map out a path of least resistance, one that relies on the same influences that everyone else is under. Instead of working against the natural flows of power, astrology can help us move with them.

There is a lot to understand when it comes to astrology, but only a small fraction will pertain to what we will explore in this book. For the most part, knowing the influences of the planets and houses will get you rather far in the craft.

The Planets and Signs

The planets are wells of power. Think of them as giant batteries that are constantly transmitting energy outward in all directions. Each planet has its own set of properties and its own type of power that it transmits. From our perspective, as the planets move around the sun, they are transiting through a set of fixed signs that are loosely based on the constellations. As they do this, they interpret the energy of that sign in unique ways and bounce it back to earth for us to deal with! Observing the transits of planets can give you added insight into when to perform a working—or perhaps when to avoid performing one.

It is believed that we take on the permanent influences of the positioning of each planet at the time of our birth and will carry these influences with us throughout life. To determine this, we would create a birth chart, which details the positions of the planets at the time we were born and drafts a set of interpretations regarding their long-term effects. To obtain a birth chart, you will need to talk to an astrologer, draft one yourself, or cheat like I did and go online to find a free copy.

Beyond working with them in this way, we can also approach the planets and the signs they travel through for aid in our magic when we have need of their energy, regardless of where or how they are stationed. The following chart details the fundamental set of properties and influences of each planet and sign. As we jump into the following chapters, you will notice that certain planets or houses lend extra strength to a working. If you are ever in doubt about what celestial or cosmic influences and correspondences to work with, check the following chart.

THE STUFF MAGIC IS MADE OF

Cosmic Force	Glyph	Influences and Properties
PLANETS		
Sun	☉	Strength, physical health and stamina, wealth, obtaining goals, achieving favorable outcomes. Associated with the element of fire. Rules Sundays.
Moon	☽	Psychic abilities, intuition, dreams, astral travel, divination, physical balance and senses. Associated with the element of water. Rules Mondays.
Mercury	☿	Knowledge, communication, wisdom, sound, vibration, travel, and transportation. Associated with the element of air. Rules Wednesdays.
Venus	♀	Love, romance, sex, beauty, business, pleasure, art, and sometimes war. Associated with the elements of fire and water. Rules Fridays.
Mars	♂	Action, movement, aggression, discipline, sex, partnership, and obstacle removal. Associated with the element of fire. Rules Tuesdays.
Jupiter	♃	Progression, success, fortune, business, luck, and boundaries. Associated with the elements of fire and air. Rules Thursdays.
Saturn	♄	Materialism and materialization, invention, ingenuity, evolution, and change. Associated with all four elements. Rules Saturdays.

Uranus	♅	Invention, thinking outside the box, revolution, refinement, divine consciousness, and potential. Associated with the element of air. Influences Saturdays.
Neptune	♆	Emotional healing, sacred visions, the arts, illusions, psychic awareness, and psychic abilities. Associated with the element of water. Influences Thursdays.
Pluto	♇	Group mind, collective consciousness, wishes, pleasure seeking, psychic abilities, and spiritual evolution. Associated with the elements of water and air. Influences Tuesdays.

SIGNS		
Aries	♈	Physicality, health, optimism, new beginnings, sports, war, and discipline. Ruled by Mars. Associated with the element of fire.
Taurus	♉	Health, healing, beauty, sensuality, and prosperity. Ruled by Venus. Associated with the element of earth.
Gemini	♊	All forms of communication, deep thought, decision making, and social life. Ruled by Mercury. Associated with the element of air.
Cancer	♋	Parenting, taking care of others, deep love, partnership, and loyalty. Ruled by the moon. Associated with the element of water.
Leo	♌	Pride, strength, creativity, social order, vanity, the arts and performance. Ruled by the sun. Associated with the element of fire.
Virgo	♍	Career, success, money management, planning, discernment, and focus. Ruled by Mercury. Associated with the element of earth.
Libra	♎	Balance in all forms, beauty, love, romance, deep thought and meditation, and the arts. Ruled by Venus. Associated with the element of air.
Scorpio	♏	Occultism and mysteries, hidden power, psychic abilities, sex, and death. Ruled by both Pluto and Mars. Associated with the element of water.

Sagittarius	♐	Adventure, travel, philosophy, language, breaking limitations, and philanthropy. Ruled by Jupiter. Associated with the element of fire.
Capricorn	♑	Leadership, long-term commitments, career goals, legacy, and tradition. Ruled by Saturn. Associated with the element of earth.
Aquarius	♒	Wisdom, escapism, timing, synchronicity, social engagement, art, and inspiration. Ruled by both Uranus and Saturn. Associated with the element of air.
Pisces	♓	Self-expression, inner knowledge, wisdom, the arts, creativity, and psychic abilities. Ruled by Neptune. Associated with the element of water.

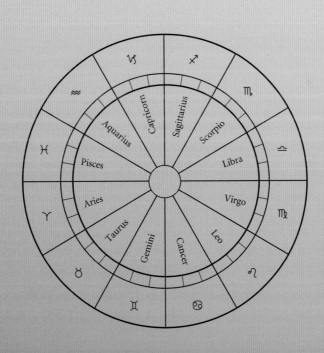

Following the Cycles of the Sun and the Moon

The sun and the moon tend to have the most impact on us daily, as they are the most directly influential "planets" (in classical astrology). When a shift occurs in them, we tend to feel the effects sooner and more dramatically than with the other planets. Additionally, both the sun and the moon are associated classically with the divine masculine and the divine feminine. The sun spends thirty days in each house, whereas the moon spends about two and half days. It takes a full year for the sun to return to its point of origin, but it only takes the moon twenty-eight days.

Many witches are taught to perform their magic specifically by using the powers of the moon. The moon does something special in that, as we see it, it waxes and wanes from new to full and back again. Coincidently, this also takes place every twenty-eight days; we refer to it as a "moon cycle."

Perform magic to gain, attract, or build something as the moon is waxing. Perform magic for wishes, devotion, and fulfillment under the full moon. As it wanes, banish and exorcize negative energies and things you no longer want. Perform cleansings and divination under the new moon.

More information about the energies present in each moon can be found by identifying the sign it is in at the time. A full moon in Pisces brings a lot of psychic energies and those related to the divine feminine to surface and is great for magic related to those things. A waning moon in Pisces would be excellent for doing work to banish nightmares and unwanted spiritual energies, whereas a waxing Pisces moon would be excellent for bringing new psychic energies into your life, such as spirit allies.

WORKING WITH SPIRITS
in Magic

"Witches and spirits go together like sunlight and solar panels" is one of my favorite sayings. We rely a lot more on spirits in witchcraft than a lot of witches care to admit. Not only are there spirits everywhere, but they always have been part of the craft. We each will be drawn to our own spirits, and I think it is important to note that no two spirits are alike, just as no two people are alike. Primarily, spirits act as our guides, teachers, and allies in magic, and on occasion they can be tempted to do things on our behalf if the right offerings are made and the right rituals are performed. The trick to building a relationship with any spirit, however, is to learn about where it comes from, what it likes, and what others have done to develop a relationship with it.

Working with spirits from outside of your own culture can be a sensitive matter. Don't let this stop you from developing a working relationship with a spirit you feel called to, but proceed with respect and caution. This doesn't mean to rush into an existing community and claim ownership; this means learning from those existing communities and discovering if you are a good fit. There is nothing worse than someone showing up and claiming power where they have not earned it. As you get to learn more about the spirit and develop a unique bond with it, you will see how it has affected other people's lives and can better judge for yourself if you want to stay for more and go deeper. When in doubt, check the internet, read a few forums, and see what type of people the spirit has in service to them—and always listen to your gut.

Listing the best spirits to work with would be like listing who I think you should be friends with, which would be a bit too weird for a book on magical workings, as generally our spiritual relationships are a bit more on the personal side. So instead of telling you who I think you should work with, instead I will list the most common types of spirits that we work with in modern witchcraft.

Spirit guides are a lot like guardian angels in that they are here to help us through life no matter what is going on, and they have the particular job of always leading us in the direction that is best for our highest good. For the most part, everyone has one primary guide; however, it is common for other guides to come and go depending on what is happening at that time in our lives. Meeting your spirit guide is something you have already done several times; you just may not have known it at the time. They speak to us in dreams, synchronicities, and symbolism. If you want a formal introduction, check out YouTube, where you will find any number of guided meditations that will help you do just that. Working with my spirit guides has been an invaluable process for me, and it has given me the opportunity to learn a lot as a witch.

Familiar spirits are not your furry animal companions but an actual type of spirit that often takes the shape of an animal. Familiars are the intermediary between us and the spirit worlds—a sort of go-to when we need to contact the unseen. They tend to be a lot like spirit guides, but the main difference is that they are not bound to only lead us in the right direction according to our highest good like spirit guides are. I give a detailed account of how to make contact with a familiar in my book *The Witch's Book of Spirits*, but the easiest way to do so is to light a black candle under the full moon and say:

> *Spirits, hear me now loud and clear:*
> *I summon a familiar who can be sincere.*
> *A companion to be by my side;*
> *A shade at noon to help me hide.*
> *I conjure a familiar here and now;*
> *To work together is my vow!*

Let the candle burn out and wait. Make a small altar somewhere for the familiar and visit it often to make contact.

Faeries are the spiritual personifications of nature—not just flowers and rocks and streams but stars and far-off galaxies as well. We mostly know them as being related to our natural world, the one we interact with every day, and each environment and geographical landscape has its own unique variety. Faeries come in all shapes and sizes and mostly prefer to be left alone. In some parts of the world, you have to ask permission from the faeries before building or horrible things might happen. There can be some truly amazing benefits to getting on their good side, however. The faeries of the home will keep your place safe and protected from fire, burglary, and discord if you treat them well. Those of your surrounding natural landscape will warn you of weather changes, earthquakes, and angry neighbors in addition to bestowing you with certain gifts if they feel warm toward you. The best offerings you can give to them are usually those made of oats, honey, milk, and beer or alcohol.

Angels are gravely misunderstood by a lot of modern witches because of their association with other religions. Classically, any helpful spirit might be called an angel; the term has been through a lot over the ages, and no one group of people gets to lay claim over it. Angels are celestial spirits who are primarily concerned with keeping the universe moving. I often refer to them as "beings of order" who, like faeries, tend to keep away from us for the most part. The lowest order of angels, known as the Ishim, is the closest to human affairs. Technically, our spirit guides would be considered a type of angel. We work with this type of angel to gain insight and wisdom into situations, especially those related to our higher selves and finding a way through chaos. Otherwise, the higher angelic orders tend to be a bit too busy keeping the universe moving to stop and pay too much attention to what us lowly mortals are up to.

Demons are real, just not in the way they are on television, unfortunately. (C'mon, who wouldn't want to see a full-on *Buffy* demon walking down Main Street and trumpeting the end of days?) In the way that angels are beings of order, demons are beings of chaos; like angels, most of them want nothing to do with us. Those we run into likely will be rooted in the psyche and are easily taken care of with the right spiritual cleansing (like the one described on page 27) and a few visits to the therapist. Demons aren't necessarily evil; they are just inharmonic to us, so they feel negative. That doesn't mean you need to be pals with them. However, it does mean you should probably stay away from them. We won't be running into any demons in this book.

The dead—especially those related to you—are, of course, all around us. They are also perhaps the easiest to talk to because they are so closely linked to the living. To communicate with the dead, all we really need to do is think of them and start talking. They are always there and always listening. In the craft we often work with our ancestors to help us with our problems or celebrate our victories; we invite them into our homes, and we visit their graves with offerings.

> *Many witches feel that the dead never truly leave; they just go on, waiting for us to call out to them. If you don't know who your ancestors are or perhaps don't feel close to them, there are plenty of dead witches such as Doreen Valiente or Victor Anderson who would love to help you out. Research them, call out to them, and make space for them.*

Gods are bit trickier to explain because each culture has a different view of what makes a god a god. For the most part, gods are different from other spirits in that their degree of influence tends to be much larger. They usually govern over the forces of life and nature and are seen as personifications of otherworldly power and influence. Nine out of ten witches I know work with and are devoted to one god or another. This isn't a necessity, but it does tend to be a natural progression for us the more we practice. Some gods make themselves more known to us than others.

WORKING WITH SYMBOLS AND SYNCHRONICITY
in Magic

Because life as we know it relies so much on perception, symbolism and synchronicity play a large part in witchcraft. Herbs and oils are tangible items; you can touch them and know they are real. Astrology allows us to study celestial and cosmic forces so we can better understand how to apply them in magic. These are things that I can quickly explain to you in a mostly rational way. Symbols, however, are a different beast altogether because they are things of personal meaning and experience. There are a select group of these things that we can all agree upon—symbols and synchronicities with meanings that have roots in our culture—but, for the most part, these matters are deeply personal in nature. As your witchcraft progresses, the meanings of symbols will change for you. You will learn to develop symbolic relationships to archetypes and totemic forces such as animals. When you are a witch, there is a never-ending evolution of symbolism and synchronicity.

Throughout this book, each of the enchantments will include various forms of symbolism and types of synchronicities to look for. Some of these will overlap; some will be entirely different than others. What matters is that you work with what speaks to you. We will explore everything from the power of numbers and colors to working with tarot to the animals, spirits, and iconography that are related to each of the enchantments. In addition to what we discuss here, it is a good idea to keep note of the things that stick out to you and how you use them in the craft.

When you are a witch,
there is a never-ending
evolution of symbolism
and synchronicity

WORKING WITH THE TAROT
in Magic

Working with tarot in your magic can be a fun and meaningful way to add a little extra oomph. Tarot makes for one hell of a divinatory system. It is packed full of symbolism as well as spiritual and material nuances. While we won't be learning the meaning of all seventy-eight cards in this book, we will be exploring ways of working with them in magic. For the most part, think of the cards as ingredients in a spell or ritual rather than only as a divination tool. Because each card is loaded with energy, we can use that energy to help propel our workings forward.

In the following chapters, you will notice there are tarot cards that have been called out for use as a correspondence in your magic. Each tarot card represents some aspect of the human experience; when the cards are interpreted in a reading, pieces of that story are woven together to form a new story, one specific to the querent. We can use this same principle to write our own story and sympathetically use the cards to help steer us in the right direction.

If you want to attract an energy, place a card symbolizing that energy on your altar. If you want to repel something, stick a card symbolizing that energy facedown on a mirror. If you want to trap an energy, use a card that symbolizes that energy and place the card in a box that is mirrored or made from iron. The possibilities are endless. As we move through this book, we will continue to explore the magical possibilities behind some of the cards.

Because each card is
loaded with energy, we
can use that energy to help
propel our workings
forward.

I have found the following cards to be particularly useful for everyday use in modern witchcraft:

The Wheel of Fortune represents fate, destiny, and the turning of the seasons. This is a card that can be used in just about any type of magic that brings about change, luck, or transformation. I use this card a lot to help alter the course of a situation if I fear it is headed in an unfavorable direction. Meditate each morning and visualize the card. When you feel like things are starting to get off-track, visualize the card and chant three times, "Wheel of Fortune, open the way; Wheel of Fortune, make my day!"

Judgement is an absolute favorite card of mine, as it symbolizes being called to our life purpose. In magic it can be used to help us better understand our path and achieve the goals related to our path that we set for ourselves. It teaches us to be independent, listen for messages from the spiritual realms, and pay close attention to our spirit guides and what inspires us. This comes in extra handy when we want to move on in life or want someone else to move on without causing them harm. Wrap their picture around the Judgement card with a white ribbon and bury it in the west at dusk.

Death gets a bad reputation because it looks scary, but the true meaning of the card is worth looking past any macabre imagery. The Death card symbolizes the end of something—not just an ending, but THE END. Whenever this card pops up in a reading, I know to prepare for something in my life to come to completion and to prepare for what comes next. In magic this card is used to finalize an energetic relationship. It won't cause literal death but rather the metaphorical death of a situation, connection, or influence. To remove an obstacle in your life with the Death card, simply write the problem in red ink on the card and then dress it with lemon essential oil by dabbing each corner. Sprinkle with cayenne pepper and then toss into a fire. (Be sure to have plenty of ventilation, as the smoke will be harmful if you breathe it in!)

The Tower is another card that looks scarier than its energy actually tends to be. Closely related to the serpent, it can represent arguments and disagreements, but it can also represent the shedding of the skin and renewal. I work with this card when I need to break negative ties or bonds, break through confusion, and even in healing magic.

If you ever feel like no one sees the real you, carry the Tower card in your pocket with a piece of citrine to encourage the beauty within to shine through.

The World is closely related to the Death card, but instead of endings, it symbolizes the completion of cycles and the start of new things to come. It can also symbolize birth and reincarnation, and it is closely linked to physical manifestation. Using a fire-safe dish, burn a candle on top of this card on Friday and visualize your desire manifesting.

The Three of Pentacles is a minor arcana card, unlike the others on this list, but it packs quite a punch energetically. It symbolizes being seen and appreciated for the work you do. Nothing is more important in life than respect, and in a world where there is a lack of respect and empathy, this card has a lot of uses. Bring it with you to work or school and keep it in your pocket to attract positive work-based attention from superiors. Tape it to the bottom of the dinner table before a meal with the family to encourage positive and productive conversation (oh-so-handy during the holidays)!

The Strength card is my all-time favorite in the deck because it represents being the underdog and rising up to be the victor. Well, that is my personal spin on it anyway. It symbolizes being strong when you have no other option but to find strength and to look at whatever it is that scares you. To me, this is one witchy card! Rising up against oppression…being strong in the face of fear…what gets witchier than that? This is another card to burn a candle over or to keep on your person when you need a little extra boost. To encourage another to be strong, make a circle with five pieces of amethyst and then place the Strength card at the center. Over the card, put a picture of the person and allow sunlight to shine over your spell. Visit this daily and gaze at the picture of the person as you send them encouraging thoughts.

We can do a lot with the cards, and as you will see, they are an invaluable tool in the craft. We will revisit them in each chapter, and in the final chapter we will take a look at cartomancy, the art of reading cards. Check out the bibliography for a list of my favorite books on the topic.

WORKING WITH NUMBERS
in Magic

Numbers come up a lot in the craft, and for good reason: they are full of symbolism. Long before numerology (a popular life path divination through numbers) was a study, people were equating numbers to the sacred and profane, and that tradition continues today. Like any other correspondence, numbers can be woven into your magic to add extra energy, but unlike the others, working with numbers as a magical act is often easier to hide in the open when needed. Usually we want to rely on more than just the numbers by adding another component to the mix. For instance, you could wear a shirt with five red roses embroidered on it to symbolize taking back your power, use seven drops of essential oil in a diffuser to lift the vibration of the room, or even place three cinnamon sticks under the bed to spice up your sex life.

Though we will get into which numbers resonate with each type of magic throughout the following chapters, here is a basic rundown of the fundamental symbolism of numbers. Though we won't get into it here, there are other numbers known as prime numbers that—like eleven, thirteen, and twenty-three, for example—cannot be divided into smaller whole numbers. This means that these numbers are highly expressive and are seen to have a particularly high spiritual vibration.

Zero is the infinite, the number that contains all numbers and symbolizes the cycles of life, death, and rebirth. In magic we use emptiness to symbolize this number. If left unfilled, the center of a circle of salt or candles, for instance, becomes the space where magic collects and coalesces. The space between our breaths, where we are neither inhaling nor exhaling, is representative of zero. Spending time in these zero spaces and experiencing emptiness allows us to truly become full over time.

One symbolizes the beginning of something new, independence from zero, and determined ambition, focus, and originality. From zero all things emerge, but what emerges first is always singularly expressed. In magic we work with the number one to represent wholeness and first steps. Lighting one candle brings focus to your workings, for example. In magic we also tend to bring several things together to create one thing. We do this when we add ingredients in a spell bottle or work clay and herbs to create a poppet. Often we work with all of these things together to form one point of focus for our magic, where we can bring focus to the otherwise separate energies of our ingredients. The number one, above all numbers, is the most important number in spell work.

Two represents duality, insight, intuition, and partnership. When we are working toward developing a relationship with someone, we always work in twos. If we are casting spells or performing magic with the intention of learning something new or gaining some sort of information, the number two is always preferred. The same can be said for magic related to truth, illusion, cultivating support, and finding peace.

Three symbolizes creativity, energetic balance, communication, and the cycles observed within life. We see three show up a lot in goddess mythology and in the work related to the soul (remember the mind/body/spirit invocation from the last chapter)? We tend to add odd numbers of ingredients to our workings, always starting with three. Add three pinches of three different kinds of herbs to a pouch and tie it three times to make a simple charm bag, for example. Light three candles to express the powers of creation and empower your workings. Burn an offering of the three holy resins—frankincense, myrrh, and dragon's blood—at any shrine to catch the attention of the presiding spirit.

Four brings stability and lends strength to magic. Four is prominent in magic because there are four primary directions, four alchemical elements, and of course four seasons. There are also four sides to the base of a pyramid and four phases of the moon. Working with the number four can draw these energies into your magic. Burn four black candles in a circle to form a protective barrier around yourself and keep your actions unseen by other witches. Write your wishes on four bay leaves and let them float along a stream or river.

Five symbolizes manifestation, protection, innovation, and projection. Perhaps the most famous number used in the craft, five can be seen in many of our sacred symbols and modern workings. There are five points on the pentacle, five primary senses, five vowels in the alphabet, and five Olympic rings. You can't go too far without running into a five in magic and the occult. Chant the names of a spirit five times to summon it. Light five candles in the shape of a star and place a doll or poppet in the center to ensorcel it. Wear a pentacle to invoke protection and safety.

Six is a bit more diabolical than the other numbers. It is often used to undo workings or reverse a spell. We see 666 as the "mark of the beast" in our culture because it symbolizes the undoing of the church and the teachings of Christ. You don't need to go that far with it unless you want to, but the same idea still applies. It has more to do with the shape of the numeral than canceling out the word of God. The shape of the numeral is counterclockwise. The number six can be used to cancel out just about any spiritual energy. To break a spell you have cast, place the remnants of the working in a circle of six black candles and recite the words from the spell backwards. (Yeah, it really works!)

To relieve yourself of the "evil eye," spin counterclockwise in a circle six times and then stomp your left foot.

Seven is a lucky number that brings positive energy wherever it goes. In magic we work with the number seven to bring perfection to our workings, gain the favor of positive spirits, and bring out the beauty in all things. For luck in gambling, leave an offering of seven new copper pennies outside of a casino or gambling facility to gain favor from the local spirits. To make yourself popular, sit in a circle of seven pink candles and chant the following seven times: "I am gorgeous; make them see. Holy Venus, use your key. What is within shall be seen about; their devotion I will not do without!" Allow the candles to burn completely.

Eight is a pretty dynamic number in that it allows us to bring our dreams and aspirations into physical manifestation. We primarily work with sets of eight in long-term magic to produce optimal results. As part of a single working, for example, burn eight candles consecutively over the course of several days to help manifest your goals in a very solid way.

Nine symbolizes the spiritual essence of the universe, wisdom, generosity, beauty, and love. When someone is "dressed to the nines," they are dressed to the highest standards. We mature for nine months in the womb before birth, also connecting this number to birth and the divine feminine. Nine is also the number most related to the process of initiation. For those seeking spiritual wisdom and insight or who are beginning a new spiritual path or course of study, it is often recommended that they take nine days to meditate and think about it before starting.

OTHER FORMS OF SYMBOLISM *in Magic*

As you can see, we work with many different forms of symbolism in our magic, but it isn't just limited to tarot cards and numbers; we also use the symbolism found in the animal kingdom, colors, and iconography. We will explore each of these as they pertain to the magic found in the following chapters, but there are a few things to live by.

The best way to honor an animal is to donate time or money toward keeping it alive **and its** environment healthy.

Working with the Animal Kingdom

The animal kingdom intersects with magic in a very cool way. In addition to being able to connect with the totemic form of the animal (sometimes referred to as a "spirit animal"), we often see animals out in the wild. Animals bring messages from the spirit world, and if we pay close attention to the animals we encounter, we just might glean special knowledge. These animals don't have to literally cross our paths—we might see them on television, on a billboard, or even in our social media feeds. If you see an animal and it calls out to you on some deeper level, research what it symbolizes and see if there is a message for you there.

In witchcraft we sometimes work with the remnants of animals who have died. Things like bones, skins, and horns often appear in spells and magical workings. This is in part because animals hold such a sacred place in our lives. Some traditions of the craft are also known to work with specific animals and have special connections to them that appear in their teachings. We recognize their importance not just as symbols, but as living beings. Spirits of all kinds find the remains of a living being more comfortable to inhabit, so even if we weren't looking to connect to the spirit of Turtle, if we had a turtle shell, it could make an excellent home for another spirit. All this being said, the emphasis on these relationships is always on conservation. Never harm an animal just to get a piece of its body for magic. Most of the bones I possess came from natural science stores, flea markets, and antique shops, or were gifted to me by hunters. The best way to honor an animal is to donate time or money toward keeping it alive and its environment healthy.

Working with Color

For the most part, there weren't a whole lot of color associations in witchcraft until we incorporated the magic of slaves. It is an often overlooked footnote in occultism that many spells and magical techniques were borrowed from freed slaves and their descendants and later integrated into our systems of magic. Color magic is one of those techniques. Modern color magic is rooted in those same principles but has grown to include elements of color therapy, design, and visual art. Every color not only symbolizes a form of energy, but also has the ability to elicit an emotional response from the person looking at it.

There are tons of colors, but here is a quick chart of the most common and their associated properties.

Colors symbolize energy and have the ability to elicit an emotional response

Color	Properties
White	Purify, bless, balance, new opportunities
Black	Protect against and eliminate negative forces/energy
Red	Strength, sexuality, love, life force, money
Pink	Friendship, physical attraction, commitment, reconciliation
Orange	Energy, new beginnings, breakthroughs
Gold	Wealth, success, opportunity, leveling up in life
Yellow	Mental clarity, inspiration, optimism, communication, confidence
Green	Healing, fertility, abundance, growth, prosperity
Blue	Peace, communication, insight, intuition, wisdom
Purple	Royalty, spiritual development, prestige, influence, importance
Brown	Grounding, the law, court cases, contracts, protection
Gray	Balance, neutrality, vision, psychism

Working with Iconography

Sometimes symbols aren't hidden but are represented in plain sight; this is the case with the iconography associated with witchcraft. To make a list of the most important symbols and icons in the craft would be impossible because not only are there more than I can count, but their importance is completely up to the person working with them. Iconography is tricky because it can be something other than a two-dimensional figure etched onto a piece of paper. The iconography found in occultism comes in the form of three-dimensional objects, living beings, and even buildings.

> Beauty—and iconography—is in the eye of the beholder.

Other Components in Magic

Different magical workings call for different magical tools and ingredients. Throughout this book we will explore several different types of spells and magical workings as well as ways to alter them so that you can tailor a working to your specific needs. Luckily for us, the majority of what we will need to perform the magic in this book can be found in nature, the home, the supermarket, at your local spiritual supply shop, or online. Thanks to the wonders of technology, few items remain hard to come by. Sometimes it is appropriate to substitute one item for another, so knowing what an appropriate substitute can be is important. In each chapter you will find lists of correspondences; when in a pinch, reference those lists for suggested substitutions. For instance, if you do not have jasmine oil for your love spell, you will find that neroli oil would be an appropriate substitute because it is listed as a correspondence for love.

The candles you select for your workings can always vary in size or shape than what you see in these pages. If you cannot get your hands on a blue pillar candle but have blue taper candles, those will do just fine! Never worry about adjusting a spell to meet your resources, but try not to adjust unless it is necessary.

The rest of what we need will come in the form of everyday items such as salt, bottles, paper, pens, and such. The most critical ingredient in magic is you; however, having basic crafting supplies like yarn, glue, clay, and carving tools is never a bad idea.

I like to reuse and recycle as much as possible, so I also make use of stuff like pickle jars, oil bottles, and brown paper bags (which make an excellent replacement for parchment paper).

*I am the force of nature
that brings magic
and change*

Another great place to find items needed for magic is out in the wild. Spend time out and about—be it in the city or in nature—and see what catches your eye. Of course, never steal and always be respectful in the manner in which you procure an item, but always be willing for the universe to present things that are charged with the magic of a specific location or item; for instance, dirt from holy ground, water from a sacred spring, gravel from the parking lot of the company you want to work for, ash from a sacred fire. These are things connected and tied to power that you may just want to have access to.

Chapter 3
LOVE MAGIC

The generations before us felt that having someone else to share their life with was the apex of true personal success, deeming those who weren't fortunate enough to find the right person a sorry soul who was truly deserving of pity. This fear was an all too familiar reality for women especially; after all, women weren't really considered to have value unless they could marry and have children of their own. It was a woman's duty to marry off, releasing the family of the obligation to clothe and feed her. If a woman stayed too long, she was going to spend the rest of her days feeling like a failure and likely never hearing the end of it. Even more frightening, what if she married someone because she had to, but there was no love, and she spent her nights sleeping next to someone she loathed or who mistreated her? Is it any wonder why love spells would have been so important?

In the twenty-first century, we have it a bit easier in some ways. We have websites and apps dedicated to introducing us to the right person. However, that doesn't always mean we are just going to run into them while browsing profiles. The odds may be higher that we can find potential partners, but it also means that because there are more options, finding the right one can be like finding a needle in a haystack the size of the planet.

Love spells are just as important today
as they were for our ancestors.

Love is a tricky thing, in any case. We have been trained by Hollywood logic to believe that the right person will find their way to us of their own accord, even if they risk great injury to themselves along the way. We still have it programmed into our minds that love from a partner is somehow going to save us from an uncertain and potentially unfortunate fate. This ideology keeps us playing by the rules of an outdated system, making it far too likely we are going to sabotage our own chance at happiness. We move from relationship to relationship, willing to settle for something that is almost (but not quite) what we want, and in return beat ourselves up when it doesn't work out. Marriage is no longer a financial transaction like it used to be. The individual's needs and desires are now at the forefront of these arrangements, and it is acceptable to get married later in life, multiple times, or even not at all. This means that when it comes to love, it is important to follow your heart and take advantage of life in the modern age.

To clear the way for successful love magic, we need to figure out a few things first. What type of love are you manifesting, and why are you doing so? Is this love romantic or platonic in nature? Do you have a specific person in mind or are you open to the possibilities? Are you seeking new love, reconciling an existing relationship, or rekindling an old romance? We need to know all these things before we start casting spells.

One of the useful things you can do is to create a "perfect partner" list. This is essentially a list of the qualities you want in a partner, but it's compiled with a twist. Instead of basic qualities like "kindness" and "a deep laugh," we are going to list traits as experiences or emotions. For instance, instead of listing "good kisser" as a quality, write down "when we kiss, I feel butterflies in my stomach." Instead of "easy to talk to," write "discussing simple and complex issues is something we do well together." As you jot these down, focus on what it will be like to actually be with your perfect partner and how you will feel as a result of those interactions. Think upon past relationships and those moments where things have gone wrong, and then draft a statement that corrects those issues with your next partner.

One of the principles found in magic is that "like attracts like," which means that if we want to attract something like love, we must first become a beacon of it or at the very least do everything we can to adjust our frequency so that we are vibrating in resonance with the frequency of love. This will give us the ability to better shape our magic as well as be open to receiving that love when the time comes. To do this, we work with herbs,

Like attracts like—
use this concept in
magic to help raise
your vibrations.

THE LOVERS

oils, magical objects, and talismans that are already infused with those vibrations so that our own can adjust accordingly. To adjust our frequency by working with correspondences is a fast and effective way of creating a path clear of magical obstruction. Everything carries its own vibration, but the following correspondences pair well with love magic.

WORKING WITH THE MINERAL KINGDOM
in Love Magic

Minerals and Gemstones: amber, amethyst, aventurine, calcite, chrysocolla, citrine, garnet, green tourmaline, jade, jasper (especially yellow, green, and ocean varieties), lodestone, malachite, opal, peridot, pyrite, quartz (clear and rose), rhodalite, rhodonite, sapphire, sunstone, tiger's eye, topaz
Metals: copper, gold

For love magic, it is best to keep one or more of these stones on your person while you are adjusting your frequency over time. Crystal magic is usually swift internally but slower to manifest externally. Each day allow the stone to touch your skin, especially near your chest, for ten to fifteen minutes while you focus on balancing and aligning your own energy. Visualize the stone acting as a filter, cleaning out vibrations associated with love that are no longer beneficial.

Each night before bed hold the stone at your navel as you say, "My body awaits a lover's touch." Move the stone up toward your solar plexus and say, "My mind awaits a lover's inspiration." Lastly, move the stone upwards to your third eye and say, "My soul awaits a lover's connection. Of these things, I am already whole but summon them still to reach my goal. A partner who inspires all of my parts; joined together, our beating hearts! I raise my signal to meet their own; through crystal vibration this magic is sewn."

Wearing jewelry made from gold or copper—especially rose gold, which is a combination of both metals—will help to adjust your

frequency by aiding in the healing of past emotional trauma as well as by strengthening your resolve surrounding what you want out of love. Metals of any kind are generally prized for their strength in magic, and when working love magic particularly, these two metals are sought after above others for their unique attributes. Gold will also attract more aggressive lovers, whereas copper will attract those of a more sensitive nature.

WORKING WITH THE PLANT KINGDOM
in Love Magic

> *Herbs and Trees:* angelica, apple, balm of Gilead, blood root, buckeye, cardamom, catnip, cherry, cinnamon, red clover, coffee, elm, fern, fig, ginger, hibiscus, lavender, orange, parsley, Queen Elizabeth root, raspberry, rose, rosemary, rue, tonka beans, vanilla, vetiver, violet, willow

Working with these plant allies, either in your garden or while cooking, is an excellent way to add extra magic into your everyday life. Grow these if possible and spend time connecting to them through meditation and intentional thought; allow the plants to tell you what you should do in order to bring love into your life. Connecting with the spirit of the plant can be done after it has been harvested and dried. However, living plants often have the most robust frequency to tap. When adding these herbs to your cooking, do so by acknowledging each herb's name and by psychically sensing its unique vibration. Once you can sense the spiritual presence of the herb, direct that energy to empower your food (and ultimately you) by adding it to whatever you are preparing and stirring it in clockwise as you visualize its essence folding into your food.

To call a specific suitor to you, plant a tea rose in a pot, placing a picture of the person you desire in the soil under the roots of the plant. Place pieces of rose quartz around the base of the stems. Allow the plant to grow naturally, and each time you water it, move the pieces of rose

A witch's heart
is not to tame

Wild and free
it must remain

quartz into new positions. This act of adjusting the stones will stir up the energy between the two of you and keep your budding relationship from getting stagnant. Once your suitor has come your way, keep the plant alive and move the pieces of rose quartz when things need to be stimulated. To call a suitor without having someone specific in mind, replace the picture with a three-times folded copy of your "perfect partner" list.

LOVE INCENSE RECIPE

Burn this incense over charcoal whenever you want to cleanse and consecrate a space or object for love magic or during spells and rituals devoted to love magic.

First powder, then combine ⅓ ounce dried rose petals, ⅓ ounce sweetgrass, and ½ ounce tonka bean. To this add 1 ounce grated honey amber resin and mix well.

Variations

Self-Love: Add ⅓ ounce each powdered bayberry and dragon's blood resin. Burn nightly before bed.

Friendship and Familial Love: Add ½ ounce powdered rosemary. Burn under the full moon to attract new friendships and strengthen family bonds.

Romantic Love: Add ⅓ ounce each frankincense and myrrh. Combine with 1 ounce honey. Spread thinly on a baking sheet and let dry until hardened (usually two to five days). Break into fingernail-sized chunks and store in a cool, dry place.

Remove Unwanted Love: Substitute honey amber with frankincense and balm of Gilead with powdered white sage. Burn under the new moon.

Reconciliation: Add ⅓ ounce powdered gravel root (queen of the meadow) and double the amount of sweetgrass used to ⅔ ounce. Burn before and during communication with a separated partner or individual.

> *Essential Oils:* ambergris, apple blossom, cardamom, carnation, catnip, cinnamon, freesia, gardenia, ginger, honeysuckle, jasmine, lavender, patchouli, plumeria, rose, rosemary, sandalwood, vanilla, water lily, yarrow, ylang-ylang

Essential oils can be applied to the body or diffused aromatically to help us cleanse our energy and align it to the vibration of the originating plant. Not all essential oils should be applied to the skin, and most should be done so only after being diluted by a carrier oil such as fractionated coconut or sweet almond. We each have different body chemistries and allergies, so be sure to do a test on your skin before applying an essential oil.

Essential oils can also be blended with other oils to create "condition oils" that can be used to influence anything they come in contact with. Oils can be added to poppets, charm bags, and fetishes, and also can be applied directly to petition papers, amulets, statues, talismans, and minerals as an act of blessing or consecration.

LOVE CONDITION OIL RECIPE

Apply this love condition oil to any spell or ritual object to instantly consecrate it with the frequency of love. Excellent for dressing candles, petition papers, love letters, etc.

To a ½ ounce bottle, add 9 drops dark patchouli essential oil, 3 drops rose essential oil, 5 drops ambergris essential oil, and 7 drops dragon's blood essential oil. Fill the rest of the bottle with carrier oil (I recommend fractionated coconut oil, grapeseed oil, or sweet almond oil).

Cap the bottle and then gently mix the oils by rotating the bottle upside down and then right-side up repeatedly until the oils have blended. The final scent will take forty-eight hours to mature and will smell differently when worn, depending on body chemistry. For extra oomph and visual appeal, charge and bless small pieces of rose quartz, rose petals, and lemongrass, and then add them to the bottle before adding oils.

A love that's true,
A love that's real—
One where both hearts
can heal

Variations

Sometimes there are specific conditions that require a small modification to the original recipe so that we can hone in on the right issues. Here are five other love condition oils that follow the same basic recipe. Make these adjustments before adding carrier oil.

To Attract the Opposite Sex: Add 5 drops catnip essential oil. Dab a few drops on each wrist daily each morning and before social activity.

For Men Who Love Men: Substitute rose essential oil with 7 drops lavender essential oil. Wear as a perfume oil or make a powder by omitting carrier oil and mixing the blend with 1 cup cornstarch or baby powder. Lightly sprinkle on floors, sheets, and the inside of your shoes to attract a potential partner.

For Women Who Love Women: Substitute patchouli essential oil for catnip essential oil. Wear as perfume or dress a violet-colored candle and burn on a Friday to attract a healthy romantic partnership.

For Trans and Queer Love: Substitute both patchouli and rose essential oils for 7 drops jasmine essential oil. Wear as a perfume or omit carrier oil and diffuse the essential blend on Wednesdays and Fridays to attract the perfect partner.

To Spice Up Sex Life: Remove rose essential oil and substitute dragon's blood essential oil with frankincense essential oil. Add a pinch of cinnamon chips or powder to the bottle. (Do not use cinnamon essential oil for this!) Add 13 drops to bath before sexual activity.

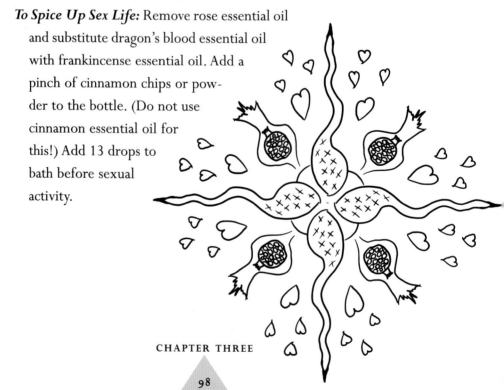

WORKING WITH COSMIC FORCES
in Love Magic

> **Signs:** Cancer, Libra, Sagittarius, Taurus
> **Planet:** Venus
> **Day of the Week:** Friday

Love magic can be done wherever or whenever, but it is powerful when performed during times of the year that are ruled by these signs. Those born under these signs are uniquely gifted in this type of magic. The moon will be of particular aid when it transits these signs, so timing your work accordingly may just give it the boost it needs to manifest in a big way.

Love magic is performed with ease when it is aligned with the vibration of Venus. This planet naturally rules over the frequency of love and therefore lends formidable strength when partnered with. Call upon the powers of Venus on Fridays.

During these times you can blend condition oils and incense, as well as make or dress candles to be used in love magic, to use in your workings later. These items will be specially charged with the right sort of energy and can be used whenever you or someone else might need them.

WORKING WITH SPIRITS
in Love Magic

> **Spirits:** Aine, Aphrodite, Astarte, Bastet, Cupid,
> the Erotes, Erzulie, Freya, Pan, St. Monica,
> St. Raphael, St. Valentine, Sappho, Venus

For those of us who don't have a specific person in mind, setting up a small altar to Cupid next to your front door is an excellent way to get attention from potential suitors. Make offerings of champagne to him once a week, and blow him a kiss each time you leave the house.

For LGBTQ+ spellcasters, finding a spirit to work with in this department can be a little rough, not because they don't exist, but because their histories have often been overlooked.

Pan is excellent for transgender, pansexual, and gay cis-male arrangements, Sappho heeds the call of lesbian and transgender lovers, and Apollo is helpful when seeking confidence in alternative relationships.

I have found that setting up an altar to them in the bedroom and lighting regular candles and incense in their names works well in getting their attention.

Regardless of the spirits you choose to work with or bring into your practice to assist in your love magic, use the sigil below to draw their attention toward the manifestation of your ideal type of love. Draw it in gold ink over the Lovers tarot card to bring a steady partnership. Draw it on a piece of parchment and slip it into your shoe to draw potential suitors. Etch it into the side of a red or pink candle to bring clarity to matters of the heart.

XOXOXO

CHAPTER THREE

WORKING WITH SYMBOLS AND SYNCHRONICITY
in Love Magic

Tarot Cards: The Empress, The Lovers, Ten of Cups, Two of Cups,

The tarot is a useful tool in magic, as each card comes psychically loaded with potential energy related to various stages or experiences in life. These cards are especially valuable when performing love magic. The Two of Cups is a great unifier for romantic love, the Lovers is precious for magic related to partnerships and reconciliation, the Empress card is useful when working toward attracting general love, and the Ten of Cups can be used to heal familial bonds.

To attract a specific lover, write their name three times on a piece of red ribbon and then tie it around the Empress card. Kiss the card three times, and after each kiss envision that it is actually them you are kissing. Say, "Empress of the Golden Road, send this to my love. Let their heart burst in rapture; inspiration from above." Keep the blessed card somewhere safe, where no one will find it, and perform the kiss-blessing aspect of the spell each night before bed until your lover comes to you.

Iconography: apple, chalice, claddagh, crown, Cupid's arrow, heart, knot, knotted Mars/Venus combinations, lock, rose, shell, triskelle, XO

In addition to being possible omens regarding your love magic, these symbols also can be used to hone in on the psychic vibration of love. Draw them or etch them into the sides of candles (see following page for icon illustrations), find and incorporate examples of them in your magic, and use them in your visualization work as representations of love.

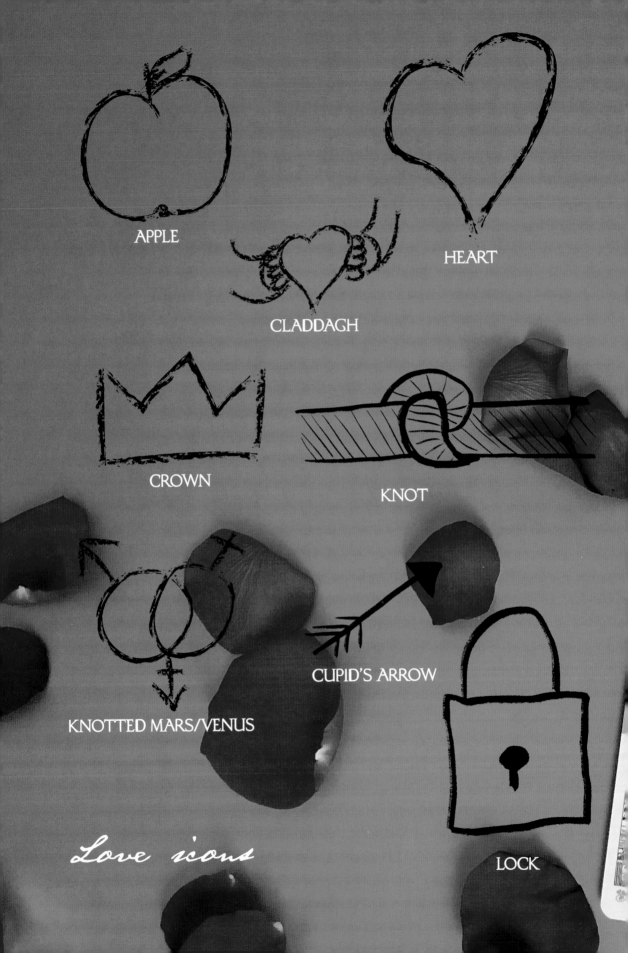

APPLE

CLADDAGH

HEART

CROWN

KNOT

KNOTTED MARS/VENUS

CUPID'S ARROW

LOCK

Love icons

X/O

CHALICE

SHELL

TRISKELLE

> *Animals and Insects:* butterfly, cat, dog, elephant, hummingbird, snail, snake, swan

Animals are messengers of symbolic and occult wisdom. Working with them as imagery or with their remains (when possible and appropriate) can be a big help in all types of magic. Pay attention if you see one of these creatures on your afternoon walk or in a dream, for they could very well be harbingers of spiritual information pertaining to your magic.

> *Colors:* green, gold, lavender, pink, purple, red, white

Candles and accessories made from materials that are predominantly these colors will act as mental and spiritual anchors for your focus and help you to better channel the psychic energies of love.

> *To heal a broken heart, tie a gold and pink ribbon around a showerhead before bathing, only removing it after nine showers and then throwing it away.*

To Reconcile with a Lover or Friend: Etch both your names on either side of a white candle and dress it with a love magic oil and carnation petals. Burn under the full moon.

To Spice Up Your Sex Life: Lay a red silk or satin sheet on the bed before intercourse and scent it lightly with patchouli water or 9 drops patchouli essential oil suspended in 12 ounces distilled water.

To Draw a Potential Lover of the Same Sex: Place a picture of them under a lavender-colored candle and then burn it in the east while chanting their name three times.

Keep an eye out for these numbers to appear in the wild as signs of your magic's progress. When performing love magic, these numbers are particularly tuned toward helping you manifest your desire, so allow your magic to have sets and patterns that contain these numbers. For example, burning two or nine candles during a ritual for love or chanting your spell ten times before releasing the energy can add subtle complexity to your work that can have significant payoff.

LOVE MAGIC CHARM BAG

To bring the right kind of love your way, create this charm bag and keep it with you in your purse or backpack. Before you leave your home each day, hold it close to your heart and take three deep breaths. Reach out with your psychic senses and wait to feel the energy from the charm bag. When you do, place it back in its compartment and keep it near. Once a week remove the charm bag and "feed" it by lighting the love incense and running the charm bag through the smoke.

Take a red square of fabric that is approximately 5 inches on all sides and in the center place the following items:

- a piece of parchment that has the first letter from every sentence on your "perfect partner" list written in red ink
- 3 copper pennies
- a tiny magnet
- 5 pinches each of dried rose petals and lavender
- 3 pinches of sweetgrass

Tie the bundle with a gold ribbon. To activate it, pass it through smoke from the love incense. As you do this, call out for help from your spirit guides and allies so that you might find the one you seek!

Carry a love charm bag with you whenever you leave the house, and slip it under your pillow at night. Traditionally, for a charm bag of this kind to remain effective, no one but the user should ever see it.

THE SELF-LOVE SPELL

In order to attract strong, passionate, fiery romantic love, the person seeking it must already feel that way on the inside. Simply put: if you can't love yourself, then the likelihood of you finding someone who can is slim. Before you cast any spell to find someone else who can love you, you have to cast a spell on yourself to do just that.

The easy way to do this is to genuinely appreciate how awesome you are. It may sound simple, but if we are going to adjust the signal you are sending out to the world, let's start with the one that says, "Hey, I'm amazing!" Think subjectively about yourself and think about what you would do for a friend who was feeling down or unlovable, and then do those things for yourself. Find reasons to invest in yourself and look for areas in your life where you deserve better, and then raise your standards in those areas. When you look at yourself in the mirror, replace the negative thoughts with positive ones and find examples of your own beauty. It is okay to look at yourself and see your own beauty, and it's okay to take pride in yourself; a witch should never forget that.

Before we can cast a spell that will cause someone to fall in love with us, we have to fall in love with ourselves. That is the trick to love magic. Do you want a partner? Want yourself first. Not only does this sort of investment in yourself completely change the game in life when it comes to how you see yourself and how others will see you, but loving yourself is one of the wickedest things you can do. It is a reclaiming of your heart and your power, and there are a few actions we can take that can indeed free us in this way. Once you learn to love yourself, the likelihood of finding the right kind of potential partner skyrockets, making that needle way easier to find. Sometimes, learning the lessons of self-love can be hard even with a little mental elbow grease, so I cast this spell a long time ago to help with that, and the results have changed my life.

> *When carving candles, paint makes for an excellent symbol relief, but do be careful regarding the paint you use. Acrylic and tempera paints work well; for an extra bit of oomph, you can add a few drops of essential oil or magnetic sand to increase attraction and magnetism.*

What You Will Need

- white firesafe plate
- gold acrylic paint
- paint brush
- the self-love sigil drawn here:
- a purple candle
- carving tool for candle
- love condition oil
- 3 pinches bayberry bark
- 3 pinches calendula flower

LOVE MAGIC

Part One: Dressing the Candle

Paint a large pentacle upon the center of the plate in gold. As this dries, carve the self-love sigil onto the side of the candle and then paint the carved section gold to accent the sigil, as seen in photo 1, left.

Once this has dried, dress it with love condition oil by liberally smearing it all over the candle.

Next, mix the bayberry bark and calendula flower together and apply half of the mixture to the sides of the candle, as seen in photo 2, left.

Part Two: Casting the Spell

Take the remaining herb mix and sprinkle it in a clockwise motion around the plate. Light the candle and recite the following incantation:

> To the one who knows my heart
> A lover from whom I'll never part.
> I awaken now a sudden flurry
> A radical love for myself that's worthy.
> Banishing all twisted beauty
> To kindle this fire is my duty.
> With this flame my love shall flow
> Pure and selfish it will grow!
> This is my will, what is best for me.
> Upon these words so must it be!

Allow the candle to burn out completely or, if needed, in stages over multiple days. When finished, take yourself out for a date!

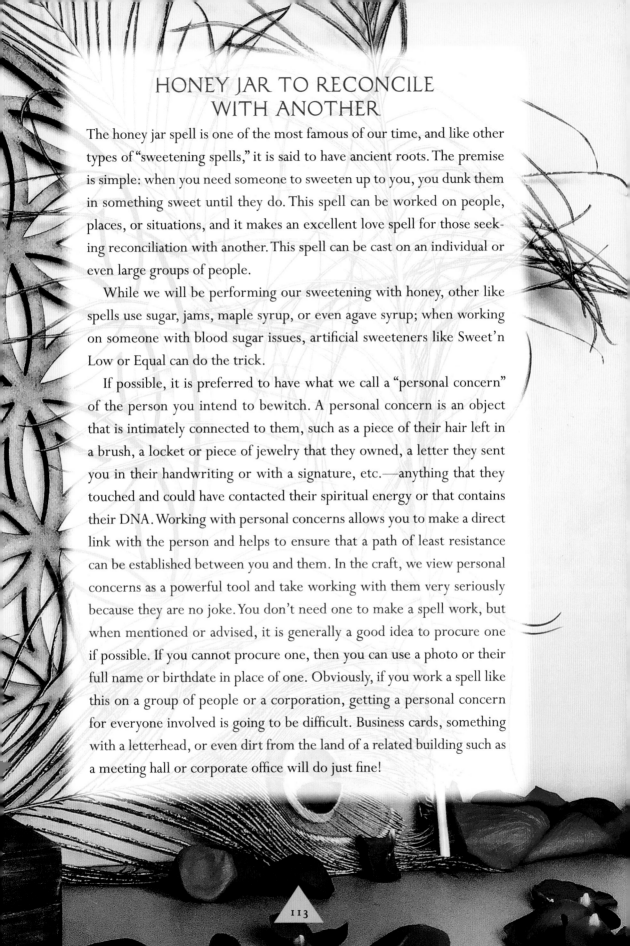

HONEY JAR TO RECONCILE
WITH ANOTHER

The honey jar spell is one of the most famous of our time, and like other types of "sweetening spells," it is said to have ancient roots. The premise is simple: when you need someone to sweeten up to you, you dunk them in something sweet until they do. This spell can be worked on people, places, or situations, and it makes an excellent love spell for those seeking reconciliation with another. This spell can be cast on an individual or even large groups of people.

While we will be performing our sweetening with honey, other like spells use sugar, jams, maple syrup, or even agave syrup; when working on someone with blood sugar issues, artificial sweeteners like Sweet'n Low or Equal can do the trick.

If possible, it is preferred to have what we call a "personal concern" of the person you intend to bewitch. A personal concern is an object that is intimately connected to them, such as a piece of their hair left in a brush, a locket or piece of jewelry that they owned, a letter they sent you in their handwriting or with a signature, etc.—anything that they touched and could have contacted their spiritual energy or that contains their DNA. Working with personal concerns allows you to make a direct link with the person and helps to ensure that a path of least resistance can be established between you and them. In the craft, we view personal concerns as a powerful tool and take working with them very seriously because they are no joke. You don't need one to make a spell work, but when mentioned or advised, it is generally a good idea to procure one if possible. If you cannot procure one, then you can use a photo or their full name or birthdate in place of one. Obviously, if you work a spell like this on a group of people or a corporation, getting a personal concern for everyone involved is going to be difficult. Business cards, something with a letterhead, or even dirt from the land of a related building such as a meeting hall or corporate office will do just fine!

> :
> :
> :
>
> *When you need*
> *someone to sweeten up*
> *to you, literally dunk*
> *them in sweetness!*

What You Will Need

- small glass jar with firesafe lid (aluminum, glass, and ceramic work fine; just avoid plastic)
- a small "personal concern"
- enough honey to fill the jar
- red ink pen
- 3 × 3-inch square of parchment paper
- corresponding love condition oil
- reconciliation incense and charcoal
- a small firesafe dish
- red candle (any size, though no larger than the lid to the jar)

Part One: Preparation

Gather your tools and ingredients. If you want to save time, often you can find glass jars of honey with metal lids at the supermarket. Otherwise, place the personal concern in the small glass jar and then fill it three-fourths of the way with honey. Set aside.

Part Two: Parchment

Using the red ink pen and parchment paper, write the name of the soon-to-be enchanted three times in a descending column in the center of the parchment square.

Rotate the square 90 degrees clockwise, then write your name three times in a descending column over the first column of names.

Here is the tricky part: you must write your intention around the two columns of names in a clockwise circle, lifting the pen from the paper only when the two ends meet. This is easiest if you write in cursive. If you do raise your pen, you will need to start this step from the beginning. For this example, we will use the phrase "Reconcile with me my love, burn for me my love, be sweet to me my love!" [see photo 1, page 116]

In each of the corners of the parchment, draw a heart and put an X through it. (X marks the spot.) Over these hearts put a dab of your chosen love condition oil. Be sure only to rotate the parchment clockwise while doing so. [2]

Part Three: Dunk

Light 2–3 pinches of reconciliation incense and run the parchment through the smoke three times, each time saying, "Open the way for love."

Fold the parchment in half toward you. Rotate 90 degrees and fold it in half toward you again. Fold it in half a third time toward you. Wash your hands after this if you find yourself without at least two clean fingers. [3]

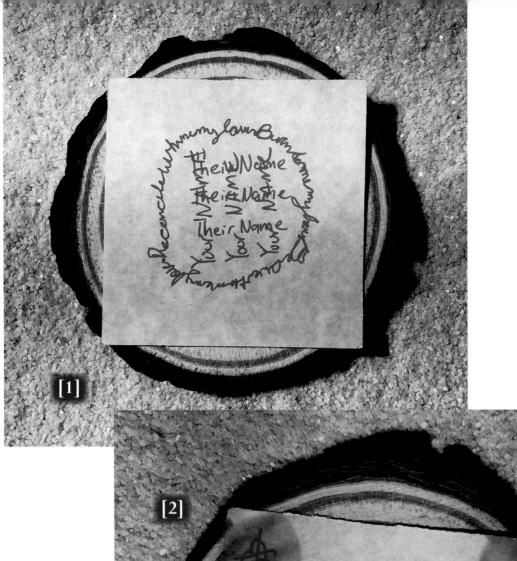

[1]

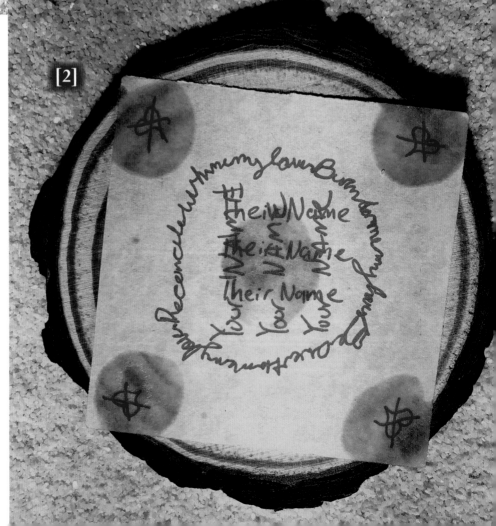

[2]

[3]

Drop the personal concerns in the honey and then pinch the folded parchment with two clean fingers and plunge it into the jar of honey, making sure to get honey on both fingers. As you lift your fingers out of the jar, immediately put them in your mouth and taste the honey.

With a bit of honey still on your tongue, say, "As this honey is sweet to me, so shall (whoever) always be!" Close the jar tightly and set aside.

Part Four: The Candle

Dress the red candle with your chosen love condition oil and a small amount of reconciliation incense. To do this, put about 5 drops of the oil in your hands and rub it all over the candle from bottom to wick. Sprinkle your reconciliation incense over the candle so that it sticks. Don't completely cover the candle with herbs, though, as that will make it a torch when lit!

Put the jar on the firesafe dish and then place the candle on the lid of the jar. It is perfectly acceptable to use a candle holder for this. I generally find that if I warm the bottom of the candle a bit, the wax tends to stick easily. There is also a product called Tacky Wax that acts as an adhesive for candles. As the candle burns, the wax will coat the jar, and that is what we are looking for long-term, so avoid using a candle holder that would prevent this from happening.

With the candle stationed on top of the jar, light it and say, "My love who has turned from me, know that I am more than you see. Come back to me to find a way; my love for you will never stray. What keeps us apart is no stronger than honey; we are better than anger, spite, and money. I want with you to reconcile, to fill your heart and make you smile. Come back to me, my lover; let us kiss, make love, and recover!"

Allow the candle to burn down completely. Again, the wax will cover the jar. Each day dress and light a new candle on top of the honey jar. Recite the spell each time and visualize the two of you getting back together again. After thirteen days you can switch to lighting a candle once a week. Do this until your lover returns and the two of you have reconciled.

KNOT MAGIC FOR LOVE

Thought to be one of the oldest forms of folk magic, knot magic (also known as cord and string magic) comes in several varieties and can be worked for just about any purpose. Usually knot magic is done to attract, bind, or bring something to you—power, money, success, influence, you name it. For our purposes, we are going to work knot magic to bring the attention of another. As I mentioned at the beginning of the chapter, there are many reasons why someone might want or need to attract a specific person. While there is no moral judgment, there are repercussions that could come from drawing the attention of the wrong person.

Aside from its intended purpose, the method used for tying knots in a cord of power will have the effect of linking you to that person. If they turn out to be someone who is ill-suited for you, you will remain bound to them. To undo this spell, you have to untie each knot, starting at the last and working your way backward, and then release the energy by burning the remains. If you do not adequately maintain or dispose of the cord once it is constructed, you run the risk of actually creating blocks that could be responsible for magical interference later as well as the creation of potential issues in related areas of your life. In this case, that means if you aren't careful and respectful of the cord and its magic, you could actually make your love life worse! Make wise choices.

What You Will Need

- 14 inches each of thin red, purple, and gold ribbon
- 7 small charms (bells or beads also work wonderfully!)
- love magic incense (of your choosing) and charcoal

Collect all of your ingredients and burn the love magic incense. Cleanse and consecrate the three pieces of ribbon and the charms by running them through the smoke three times while chanting "Bad, bad, clear away; love, love, come my way!" with each passing.

Tie the ribbons together about three inches into their length, making sure that the pieces begin and end at the same point. This will ensure that they stay together. As you do this, say, "By the knot of one, this working has begun!"

Braid the ribbon together for one inch. Place one of the charms onto the middle ribbon and then take the left ribbon in one hand, the middle and right in the other, and tie them together in a knot. As the ribbon slides into the knot, say, "By the knot of two, this spell will come true!"

Repeat step three six more times, braiding for one inch and then tying a charm with a knot. With the third knot, say, "By the knot of three, all hear my decree!" With the fourth knot, say, "By the knot of four, this magic opens the door!" With the fifth knot, say, "By knot of five, this spell is alive!" With the sixth knot, say, "By knot of six, this (man, woman, person, group, etc.) I fix!" With the seventh knot, say, "By knot of seven, a deed from hell or heaven!" With the eighth knot, say, "By knot of eight, I braid this fate!"

Braid the ribbon together for one more inch and then tie a knot without a charm. As you do this, say, "By knot of nine, (insert name here) is mine!" while you visualize that person kissing you or a group welcoming you.

Wrap this around a crystal or a wand and put it on your altar for seven nights. Pick it up often and visualize the person kissing you as you say, "Nine knots make them mine!"

After seven nights, wrap the cord on your ankle or wrist, around your neck as a necklace, or braid it into your hair to keep it on you. You will want to wear it around this person as often as possible. When you are not using it, wrap it around a crystal or a wand.

Knot magic is ancient and time tested, making it one of the most preferred ways to attract a lover.

Chapter 4
HEALING MAGIC

ealing magic is an incredibly diverse field of study and application—so diverse that it is rare many witches would agree on what works best and what doesn't work at all. Some of us favor energetic healing over working with herbs, some of us work with folk remedies, others exclusively with the application of essential oils, etc. No matter the ailment, there is some form of healing magic associated with it.

The number one rule of healing magic is that energy follows the path of least resistance. This means that healing magic should be something that is done in concert with good ol' Western medicine. Trust me, I avoid going to the doctor like most witches avoid church. I have had things go wrong, I have been misdiagnosed, I have lost people during medical procedures, and I have seen people I love wither away in a nursing home. It takes a lot to get me to a doctor, but one thing the spirits have taught me over the years is that they always want to use the fastest route toward the end goal. Ninety-nine percent of the time, Western medicine is the fastest way to that. This is to say that if you are working with a physician, don't stop or forgo treatment because you cast a spell or had energy healing performed. Healing magic works best when it can ride on the back of traditional treatments. It is always better to have ensorcelled the antibiotics than to have never taken them at all. For that matter, it is better to cast a spell to ensure you receive the correct diagnosis than to avoid seeking medical attention. Remember, you are a witch; you never have to walk into a big situation without backup.

APPROACHES TO HEALING

Healing magic is hard because there is no one-size-fits-all approach to it. There are so many methods that it can quickly become overwhelming for any witch, new or sage, to know where to start and what actually works. The difficulty comes from having to approach two problems simultaneously, each of which can have their own set of variables that need to be individually tackled.

For healing magic to be successful, we have to treat the cause and the symptom, both of which are going to be rooted in both physical and spiritual planes. To do this, we need to know what we are up against, and sometimes that means we need to cast a spell to ensure proper diagnosis.

If you have performed healing work before and it wasn't as effective as you had hoped, I would advise that you learn about the issue you are working to cure or ease the discomfort through a scientific and medical lens. All it takes is a Google search and you will be able to learn about its life span, the way it interacts with the body, what it looks like, and what the effects are that it will have on the body. Get a real sense from an anatomical and physiological level of what it is you are working with. You don't need to be a doctor to know what a cancer cell looks like, and knowing what it looks like is essential when you are combating it. Here are a few of my notes on treating some of the more common issues.

Notes on Magically Treating Illness

For everyone suffering from a cold, there is a spirit or energy that is on the other side associated with their ailment. The body has to handle the physical nature of the cold, but the soul has to deal with the spiritual nature of the cold. In these instances we need to approach healing not just to help the body restore itself, but we also might need to banish that spirit so the body can actually do what it needs to do to heal in the first place. When someone is ill, it is a good idea to perform a cleansing both on them and the space where they are recuperating. My preferred method for this is to have the person take a cleansing bath, made by combining 1 cup sea salt with 13 drops each of tea tree, eucalyptus, and white sage essential oils. To cleanse the space, I diffuse these same oils in an oil burner three times a day until the illness is gone.

Notes on Magically Treating Disease

There are times when we find we have a disease like diabetes, heart disease, or multiple sclerosis and are faced with long-term symptom management. Healing the body will be difficult in these circumstances because the body is literally working against itself. Again, lesser spirits looking to take advantage of the situation are of concern, but of more importance is helping the body reprogram itself. To do this, you would need a thorough understanding of the body and its processes.

If you are going to treat a disease or disorder, you must know everything you can about it. You also need to know everything about the body in relation to that problem. Before you work with herbs, you must know how they interact with the body and any possible medications. Herbs are strong medicine and can counteract certain other treatments. So, in addition to healing magic, the healing process requires some specifically non-magical education.

Diseases are often tackled by therapeutically working with crystals and essential oils. Bloodstone is especially good for the resolution of diseases that affect the blood, adrenal system, liver, lungs, and heart. It is also known to assist the body's immune system during immunotherapy and for assisting in the growth of damaged tissue. On the other hand, when working to heal tumors and cancers, it is not a good idea to work with a crystal that stimulates the growth of anything! Instead, we would want to work with fluorite, as it is known to assist healing on a cellular level and can help with those harder-to-treat issues.

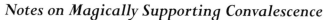

Notes on Magically Supporting Convalescence

Sometimes things just go wrong, like we get into an accident or we get older and our bodies just start to slow down. There aren't any spirits or energy necessarily associated with the cause of these things, but there are spirits that will take advantage of the situation. I mean, we wouldn't expect a lion to give up on making an easy meal out of a lame gazelle, so we can't fault them for trying to survive themselves. In cases like these, we would want to help the body regenerate, but we would also want to draw in positive spiritual energies and protect against those lesser spirits that might impede the process. Again, keeping the area cleansed is essential for this, but we also want to call upon spiritual protectors to make this happen. Archangel Raphael is a favorite spirit to work with for this. Light a green candle and summon his aid by saying,

> *Archangel Raphael, teacher of healers, protector of the ill and*
> *weak, come to our aid and drive away the wickedness. Make this*
> *space pure and let it be cleansed in your name. As this candle*
> *burns, so shall you be a beacon in this place. Blessed be!*

Crystals are supplements for the energy body

Working with the following correspondences will help you to approach healing magic with confidence, as they are each imbued with this power. If you find yourself doing a lot of healing, it might be best to create an altar just for this work. There you can focus on your healing work without it being disturbed by other energies you might want to work with on your main altar. At the very least, keep a section of your altar where the tools you use for healing can all stay close to one another. It is also a good idea to cleanse each instrument or tool, as well as yourself, before and after performing a healing of any kind. This will ensure that unwanted energies don't cause a problem for you later down the road.

WORKING WITH THE MINERAL KINGDOM
in Healing Magic

Minerals and Gemstones: agate, amethyst, amazonite, apatite, aventurine, bloodstone, carnelian, celestite, citrine, fluorite, garnet, geode, hematite, Herkimer diamond, jade, jasper, lapis lazuli, moonstone, quartz (especially rose and clear varieties), shungite, topaz, tourmaline (especially black and green varieties)
Metals: gold, silver, stainless steel, titanium

As I mentioned earlier, crystals are excellent tools when used in healing magic. I often think of them as supplemental energy for the energy body in the way that vitamins are supplemental to the physical body. To keep your body healthy and to assist in overall energy levels, make a crystal elixir and drink it daily. A crystal elixir is made by placing a stone in a jar with fresh (usually distilled or spring) water and then allowing it to charge in sunlight for an entire day. Once the twenty-four hours are up, the water is believed to be charged with the power of the stone.

You can drink it or bathe in it, making sure to remove the stone before using the elixir. Not all stones are safe to do this with, however. Research the stone before you work with it in this way, as some possess toxins that can be harmful if ingested. Those I list here are safe to use.

> Work with Herkimer diamond for an all-purpose health boost, apatite when you need to lose weight, garnet to assist in reproductive health, and tourmaline to assist in the mending of bones.

Wearing jewelry made from any of the metals listed here will assist you as a healer in connecting your mind and spirit with the physical realm. Silver is a favorite of mine to work within healing magic, especially colloidal silver. Colloidal silver is made when electricity passes through a piece of silver that is suspended in (usually distilled) water. The silver releases small particles into the water, resulting in a solution that is roughly 30–50 percent silver particles. This is not something you want to make at home because it can be quite dangerous to make. Luckily, we can buy it in just about every health food store or vitamin shop. In addition to holding on to an energy charge that can be ingested, it is known for fighting infection and assisting the immune system. Under the full moon, charge the colloidal silver by allowing moonlight to enter the bottle and reciting the following charm three times:

> Silver light, silver waters
> Silver charmed by moonlight.

Take as instructed by the manufacturer.

WORKING WITH THE PLANT KINGDOM
in Healing Magic

> **Herbs and Trees:** aloe, angelica, apple, avocado, bay, bittersweet, black cohosh, boneset, burdock, calamus, calendula, cannabis, chamomile, cinnamon, coriander, cucumber, dandelion, dill, echinacea, elder, eucalyptus, fig, garlic, ginger, goldenseal, green tea, heal-all, hops, horehound, juniper, lavender, lime, lemon, lemon balm, life everlasting, marshmallow, master root, mint, mugwort, mullein, myrrh, nettle, oak, olive, peony, pine, poppy, rosemary, self-heal, turmeric, white willow bark, wintergreen, witch hazel

We work a lot with the plant kingdom in healing magic, both for its traditional and medicinal purposes. If you are someone who takes herbal supplements, connect to the indwelling spirit of the herb by holding the supplement in your hands and visualizing a white light emerging from its center. Take a deep breath, blow over the supplement, and see this light grow larger and then fade as if kindling the coals of a fire. This will activate the magical properties of the herb before you take it.

Otherwise, we can work with herbs to create balms and salves, and we can brew teas to assist in the healing process.

Herbs such as eucalyptus, mint, lemon, and tea tree— which are often used as flavors or components in over-the-counter medications—have ancient origins as healing allies.

HEALING INCENSE

Burn over charcoal to imbue your workings with the power of healing or as a working of its own to encourage general healing in the home.

Powder and then combine ⅓ ounce chamomile, ½ ounce sweetgrass, and ¼ ounce lavender. To this add ⅓ ounce powdered frankincense resin and mix well.

Variations

Mental Healing: Add ⅓ ounce rosemary and substitute frankincense with dragon's blood resin. Burn before and after counseling sessions or shadow work to relieve frustration and aid the mind in healing.

Deep Emotional Healing: Add ⅓ ounce calendula and substitute frankincense with myrrh. Make this under the new moon, if possible, and burn anytime.

Long-Distance Healing: Add ¼ ounce eucalyptus and ⅓ ounce lemon balm. Burn when working with someone who is not physically present or to empower healing dolls.

Ward Against the Spirits of Illness: Substitute chamomile with white or desert sage; omit sweetgrass. Burn during the new moon and chant six times, "Begone, spirits who would bring sickness and disease; my witch power wards against you with ease!"

Disconnect from Patient: Add ⅓ ounce myrrh; omit sweetgrass. Burn after a healing to disconnect from a patient and their issues. Pass through the smoke twice and then stomp your right foot and say, "Let it be finished for now."

My witch power wards against sickness with ease

> **Essential Oils:** anise, black pepper, camphor, carnation, citron, clove, coriander, cypress, eucalyptus, gardenia, grapefruit, juniper, lavender, myrrh, oregano, palmarosa, pine, rose, sandalwood, spearmint, tea tree

HEALING CONDITION OIL RECIPE

Essential oils have both medicinal as well as metaphysical properties. Working with both sets of properties in mind is an important aspect of healing magic. Like herbs, not all essential oils are good for you, and you may have allergies to them. Often those with allergies will notice a higher degree of irritation when working with the essential oil of a plant than simply the plant itself. Again, do your research. Before you apply any oil to a large patch of skin, test it out first on a small patch of skin. You can work with this oil both medicinally and as a condition oil.

To a ½ ounce bottle, add 7 drops oregano essential oil, 7 drops lavender essential oil, 13 drops frankincense essential oil, and 10 drops tea tree essential oil. Fill the rest of the bottle with carrier oil. (You can also add this oil blend without carrier oil, using 16 ounces of warm distilled water to make a skin and wound wash with antimicrobial, antibacterial, antifungal, and anti-inflammatory properties. Only use this method with this recipe.)

Variations

Assist the Mind During Healing: Add 9 drops rosemary essential oil. Diffuse during and after a healing session or when journaling.

Assist the Heart During Healing: Add 9 drops cypress essential oil and substitute the tea tree essential oil with grapefruit essential oil. Diffuse during the healing session and at night before bed.

Assist the Body During Healing: Substitute tea tree essential oil for cypress essential oil and add 5 drops clove essential oil. Diffuse in the morning as well as during a healing session.

Promote Healing Wisdom: Substitute tea tree essential oil with dragon's blood essential oil. Wear on the body during healing work or study.

Aftercare for Energy Healers: Omit tea tree and frankincense oils. Add 9 drops each myrrh essential oil and chamomile essential oil. Wear on the skin or omit carrier oil and suspend in 12–16 ounces distilled water and use in a spray bottle as a mist.

WORKING WITH COSMIC FORCES
in Healing Magic

Signs: Aquarius, Scorpio
Planets: Earth, Mars, Mercury, Moon, Sun
Days: Monday, Tuesday, Wednesday, Sunday

Never let timing get in the way of performing a healing spell when you need to. However, if you can plan to do your workings when Aquarius or Scorpio have a prominent position in the heavens, you are sure to find that they are done with ease, especially when the sun and moon transit them. Those born under these signs are likely to be gifted healers as well.

There are five planets and four days that stick out as being sources of strength for healing. Perform workings to heal the mind and soul on Sundays and Mondays in the name of the sun and the moon. Those workings related to weight management, exercise, and physical strength should begin on Tuesdays, when Mars is the ruler.

On Wednesdays perform magic for mental health and emotional healing; in addition, it's a good day to seek new treatment or communicate with medical staff.

Use the black sigil
below to assist in healing
magic. It will focus the
collective energy of your spirit
allies and direct it toward
the healing process.

WORKING WITH SPIRITS
in Healing Magic

Spirits: Agwu, Apollo, Asclepius, Aset, Ashvins, Athena, Brigid, the Dagda, Dianus, St. Dymphna, Eir, Freya, Gabriel, Gaia, Gwydion, He Xiangu, Heka, Hippocrates, the "Hooded Spirits," Hygeia, Mannanan, St. Peregrine, Raphael, Thoth

Set up a small altar to one of these spirits or include them on your current altar. Make offerings to them weekly and before any healing magic is performed. Ask for guidance and intervention on your behalf regarding health concerns. As mentioned earlier, I find Raphael to be a big help with healing, and Raphael loves to work with witches. I keep a candle burning for this spirit regularly and make offerings of healing incense and white wine when a great act of healing has been performed with Raphael's aid.

The power to heal someone energetically is a natural gift of the witch power; we just have to learn to access it. To heal yourself, visualize a white flame pouring down from the sun or moon (it is the same light!) and entering the top of your head. See this light pour down into your heart, where it turns green and then begins to cycle through the body. Continue to do this for at least one minute. When finished, take a deep breath, disconnect from the sun/moon, and allow the energy within the body to be absorbed.

To heal another, see the white fire enter the top of your head, move downwards to the heart, and turn green. Instead of allowing it to cycle through the body, visualize it splitting into two streams of green fire, both exiting through the palms. Hover your hands six to ten inches from the body of the person you are healing and project the green flame into their body. When finished, see the two streams stop pouring from the heart and visualize only white fire moving through your own body for one minute, then disconnect and allow the energy within the body to be absorbed.

WORKING WITH SYMBOLS AND SYNCHRONICITY
in Healing Magic

> **Tarot Cards:** Death, Four of Swords, Six of Swords,
> The Star, The Sun, Temperance

The tarot can be used in healing magic to represent the type of healing required. We draw upon the archetypical influences of the cards to paint pathways for our healing energy to manifest.

As they sleep, the Death card can be placed under the pillow of someone suffering from illness. In the morning remove the card and burn it to banish the affliction. The Four and Six of Swords both represent rest and recuperation and should be placed on the altar during convalescence to keep the person being healed safe from stress and worry. The Star and Sun cards can both be worked with to encourage mental health and clarity, as well as to assist in the relief of depression or anxiety. The Temperance card can be placed in the medicine cabinet to ward against complications with medicines.

> **Numbers:** 1, 3, 5, 7, 9

When performing healing magic, it is ideal to incorporate these numbers, as they are known for bringing luck in such workings.

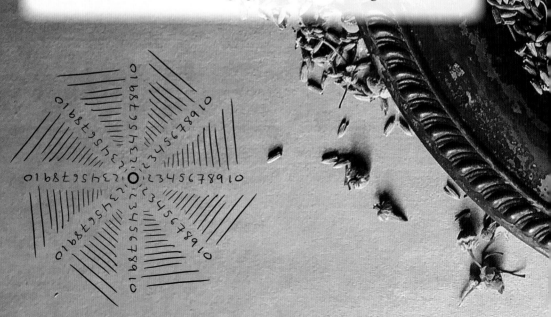

A SPELL TO RECEIVE THE CORRECT DIAGNOSIS

The right diagnosis can save you time as well as remove potential obstacles on the road to healing. On occasion, while doctors do their best to identify and treat a problem, any number of delays may keep them from finding the solution that works for you. Many people avoid the doctor altogether due to fear of misdiagnosis.

Cast this spell before a visit with your MD
to ensure that you receive the right diagnosis
as well as the correct course of treatment.
This simple spell incorporates numbers
associated with healing magic, and all
you need is a piece of wood to knock on.

On a piece of wood, knock one time and say, "Once for the truth." Knock three times and say, "Three for each soul." Knock five times and say, "Five for the answers to make me whole!" Lastly, knock seventeen times and say:

> *Spirits that are true and wise,*
> *Be my aid and be their eyes.*
> *Find the answers and the way*
> *Diagnose and then convey.*
> *What is ailing, what is wrong;*
> *What keeps me from being strong?*
> *To my doctor this impart*
> *All your wisdom from the start!*

> *Animals and Insects:* bear, bee, boar, buffalo, cicada, crane, dog, dove, eagle, hummingbird, peacock, raven, salmon, snake, toad, whale

The animal kingdom has a lot of magic to share with us, and any one of these animals can be worked within your healing magic. I have great luck working with the spirit of Bear and Peacock. Bear helps with bone, muscle, and blood concerns, as well as anything related to physical strength or longevity. Peacock helps with the liver, pancreas, adrenals, and the sexual organs. In addition to this, Peacock is a great help to those who are fighting addictions. Wear a charm with one of these animals, meditate or journey to meet them, and incorporate them into your workings.

> *Colors:* brown, gold, green, iridescent, light blue, red, silver, teal, violet, white

Candles and accessories made from materials that are predominantly these colors will act as mental and spiritual anchors for your focus and will help you to better channel the psychic energies related to healing. Tie a teal ribbon on the door of one who is sick to invite swift recovery. Wear red when you are healing from any ailment that caused you to feel physically weak or drained. To ease pain, place a violet-colored blanket or shawl around your shoulders and sleep.

> *Iconography:* bowl of Hygeia, caduceus, healing rays, lotus, purify, ram's head, red cross, rod of Asclepius, serpent, strength of the Goddess, triquetra, Uruz rune

In addition to being possible omens regarding your healing magic, these symbols also can be used to hone in on the psychic vibrations related to healing. Draw them or etch them into the sides of candles, find and incorporate examples of them in your magic, and use them in your visualization work as representations of good health, longevity, and healing.

CADUCEUS

BOWL OF HYGEIA

LOTUS

RAM'S HEAD

RED CROSS

Healing icons

ROD OF ASCLEPIUS

SERPENT

STRENGTH OF
THE GODDESS

TRIQUETRA

URUZ

HEALING RAYS

PURIFY

Heal the body
heal the mind
Heal afflictions
of all kind

HEALING SALVE

We have been making healing salves for longer than anyone really knows, but the practice has gotten easier with time. Healing salves once were made with animal fat and other ingredients that can be harmful to the skin. Nowadays we can make entirely vegan options that are much better for the skin and use easier-to-obtain ingredients. Healing salves are made by infusing oils with herbs and then blending that infused oil with beeswax and other ingredients to make a thick herbal butter that can be easily applied to the skin.

What You Will Need

FOR PART ONE

- 12-ounce clear glass jar with lid
- ½ ounce comfrey leaves
- ½ ounce rosemary
- ½ ounce lavender
- ½ ounce chamomile
- 8–10 ounces fractionated coconut oil (or other carrier oil)
- cheesecloth or a fine strainer
- 500–900 milliliters vitamin E oil (optional)

FOR PART TWO

- 1 ounce beeswax
- 8 ounces herbal-infused oil from part one
- 1 ounce shea or cocoa butter (optional)
- 7 drops lavender essential oil
- 5 drops peppermint essential oil
- 3 drops tea tree essential oil
- six 4-ounce (dark or frosted) glass jars or metal tins with lids

Part One: Infuse the Oil

Fill the clear glass jar with the dried herbs and then fill the jar with carrier oil. For this, I recommend using fractionated coconut oil, which will lend itself to a super smooth final product. Seal the jar tightly.

Put this jar in a window and allow the sun to warm it daily for thirteen days. Each day pick up the jar and shake it while you chant, "Heal the body, heal the mind, heal afflictions of all kind." You will likely notice that the herbs will absorb some of the oil after several days. This is fine as long as they themselves remain covered. If you need to, add more oil. The oil should take on the scent of the herbal mix after thirteen days.

After the thirteenth day, strain the oil with cheesecloth or a fine strainer, making sure that the herbs are separated. Be sure to squeeze and release as much of the oil that was absorbed by the herbs as possible. Discard herbs.

Store the infused oil in a dark container or, if using the same jar you used to infuse the oil, be sure to store in a dark place. Add about 500–900 milliliters vitamin E oil to the mix to prolong shelf life if needed. This oil should be stable for up to a year on its own.

Part Two: Make the Salve

In a double boiler or small slow cooker, combine 1 ounce beeswax with 8 ounces of the herbal-infused oil from part one. Allow the wax to melt into the oil, stirring occasionally. For a little extra awesome, add 1 ounce shea or cocoa butter.

As soon as the wax is melted and has been incorporated, remove the mixture from the heat and allow it to cool until you start to see it solidify on the top. When this happens, add the essential oils and mix well, then pour the salve into the small (4 ounce) glass jars or metal tins to cool and thicken. Makes roughly 9–10 ounces.

Apply healing salve to light burns, abrasions, bug bites, and other minor skin irritations.

Store in a cool, dry place. If using a clear or frosted container, refrigerate or store in a dark place to prolong shelf life. This is stable for at least one year.

SERPENT CANDLE

The serpent candle spell can be performed on any person who needs healing. Working with powerful serpent energy, this candle stimulates regeneration in the body and the shedding of ailments. You don't need to wait for a specific day, but this is usually best performed at dusk. Burn as often as you can until the ailment is cured. The candle, once carved and dressed, will be symbolic of the rod of Asclepius in our working.

Like all candle spells, it is important to keep an eye on them while burning and to pay attention to how the candle burns. Clicking and popping from the wick can indicate that there are blockages or things impeding the success of the spell. A tall flame can indicate the need for attention from a medical doctor.

What You Will Need

- a picture of the person being healed or a piece of parchment with their full name
- firesafe dish
- white pillar candle
- carving tools
- ½ ounce ground cloves, powdered
- healing condition oil
- healing incense and charcoal

Part One: Carve the Candle and Prepare the Plate

Put the picture of the person to be healed on the center of the firesafe dish and set aside.

Using your carving tools, carve two parallel lines that wrap around the candle to make the body of the snake. I like the body to be roughly one-third the size of the candle's diameter. Discard the extra wax.

Fill the snake body by carving a diamond pattern of overlapping perpendicular lines that are at least 1 centimeter in size.

Part Two: Dress the Candle and Cast the Spell

Gently rub the powdered cloves into the grooves where you have carved the candle. This should fill in the carving to better reveal its shape and features. Wipe away any excess with a napkin if needed.

Next, gently coat the candle in healing condition oil, doing your best not to smudge too much of the clove.

Light the incense. Pass the candle through the smoke three times, and each time say, "Serpent, rise! Heal this soul. Shed the skin and make them whole!"

Put the candle on top of the picture on the firesafe dish. Wipe your hands clean.

Take three deep breaths and focus on the wick of the candle. Visualize a serpent slowly crawling up the base along your carving, repeat again three times, "Serpent, rise! Heal this soul. Shed the skin and make them whole!"

Visualize the serpent's head emerging through the wick, light the candle, and then recite this incantation:

> Heal the wounds, heal the flesh
> Heal the mind and keep it fresh.
> Serpent, rise from down below
> Burn you bright and burn you slow.
> Regenerate the body and comfort the soul
> Shed your skin and make them whole!

Allow the candle to burn out completely on its own. If you need to leave it unattended, put it out by snuffing it, not by blowing it out, and relight as soon as possible.

Serpent, rise!
Heal this soul

Shed the skin and
make them whole

HERBAL HEALING POPPETS AND DOLLIES

Another way to heal someone is through the sympathetic act of creating a miniature version of them in the form of what we call a poppet or dolly. These can be used in magic to represent the person we intend to bewitch, and while it is always preferred to have a personal concern of theirs, it isn't necessary. If you cannot procure a personal concern, then use a picture of the person and write their name four times on the back.

Some poppets are made from fabric, others clay or wax, and some of the oldest were made from simply tying sticks together. Many witches and pagans still make corn dollies, a traditional European poppet made from straw or maze husks, which honors the spirits of the harvest. Some witches choose to work with porcelain or store-bought dolls and then dress them up as the intended bewitched.

Our poppet will be made using fabric and herbs and will require a small degree of sewing skill. It doesn't matter if you hand or machine sew this project, as long as the doll will seal in the end. The fabric you choose doesn't matter as long as it represents that person to you. If possible, the ideal personal concern to use in this spell would be a piece of fabric from an article of clothing owned by this person. When in doubt, working with any of the colors listed in this chapter will do!

*By chamomile,
lavender, and
rosemary,
I conjure a doll
to soothe worry*

Poppets are used
in magic to represent
the person we intend
to bewitch.

What You Will Need

- two 7 x 10-inch swatches of fabric
- needle for sewing
- white thread
- scissors
- paper to trace pattern
- copal resin
- chamomile
- lavender
- rosemary
- healing condition oil
- healing incense and charcoal
- a personal concern or photo
- 3 green votive candles
- 3 white-headed pins

Awaken now, idol— a perfect clone

Part One: Make the Poppet

Draw a simple doll or gingerbread figure of your choice on a piece of paper and cut out the figure. Use this as a stencil to trace and cut out the pattern on the two pieces of fabric so that you have two identical fabric cutouts.

Sew the two pieces of fabric together along the outer edge, leaving a 1-inch hole on the side for stuffing.

Stuff the doll with the personal concern or photo as well as equal parts chamomile, lavender, rosemary, and copal. Sew the 1-inch hole to close the doll.

Part Two: Empower the Poppet and Perform the Working

Dress the three candles with healing condition oil and healing incense.

Place the candles in an upside-down triangle large enough for the poppet to fit in. Surrounding this, make a thin circle of lavender flowers.

Light the healing incense and then the candles and run the poppet through the smoke ten times, each time declaring that the doll now represents the intended bewitched. "This doll represents (so and so)!"

Put the doll in the center of the triangle and then recite the following charm:

> *By chamomile, lavender, and rosemary*
> *I conjure a doll to soothe worry.*
> *From stitch to stitch, with copal heart*
> *I summon the powers to watch its start.*
> *Awaken now, idol—a perfect clone*
> *Just as if you were flesh and bone!*

Allow the candles to burn out, and once they have, your poppet is empowered and ready to use!

Once your poppet is alive, you must keep it that way by "feeding" it weekly. Do this by passing it through incense smoke and making the occasional offering of clear liquor or Florida water.

To perform a healing with the doll, rub a bit of the healing condition oil of your choosing on the head of a white pin as you form the intention for that particular ailment to be healed and disappear.

Poke the needle end of the pin into a corresponding part of the doll. For instance, if it is a headache, put a pin through the part of the head where the pain is noticed. If it is to help with emotional healing, the head or heart areas are great places to focus energy with the pin. Continue to do this until all three pins are used in this way.

To finish the session, pass the doll through smoke again three more times, and as you do so, say, "(So and so) is healed by the witch's touch!" each time.

Store the poppet somewhere where it will not be touched by anyone else and where the pins can remain until you need to perform the working again.

Each time you use a pin, simply dab a bit of the oil on the tip and let it do all the work. There is no need to cleanse the needle in between uses on the same doll.

Chapter 5

PROTECTION
MAGIC

The sad truth is that in life we require protection—and as a witch this is doubly so—from any number of things that might be thrown at us. Not only do we need to protect ourselves from the things an average person would, such as severe weather, theft, violence in the streets, other people on the road, etc., but we also need to keep ourselves safe from matters of a more preternatural origin. Spirits, other witches, and even low-frequency energy from your surroundings can all become a problem when you aren't adequately prepared.

There are thousands of different ways to protect yourself magically, which is a practice known as warding. While some of us take this work lightly, others feel much differently about it. I am one of those witches that takes warding magic very seriously, as I have learned over the years that I am prone to accidents (generally of a comedic nature, thankfully) as well as attracting the attention of people who don't always want the best for me. I have also helped a lot of clients out of bad situations that could have been avoided with a little warding magic.

Now, naturally we can't protect ourselves from everything, and when our time comes, our time comes. But we can do a lot to keep unwanted things from happening or developing in our lives. Like most magic, protection magic requires us to both alter the likelihood that we will encounter X while simultaneously shielding ourselves from X if it were to occur. The concept is to do everything in our power to keep debris from hitting the ship, but, if it does, the hull needs to be protected enough that it won't take on critical damage. No, we don't want to get in a car accident, but it is better to walk away with a sprained ankle than not at all; trust me, I know from personal experience.

Let's get another thing straight as well: magic only works when you get out of its way. You could cover yourself in protection sigils and have a sparkling daily practice, but if you surround yourself with shady people, your life is going to be full of shady activity. You must keep the likelihood of unsavory behavior at a minimum if you are going to be successful. I am in no way blaming a victim for the fate that befalls them—protection magic is all about keeping us from becoming victims of each other and of fate—but we must remember that it is all about increasing or decreasing the odds that something will happen. If we are going to invest in behavior that will increase the likelihood that something will happen, it is merely going to be more likely to happen.

I hope that for most of us the need for protection magic is limited to the normal, but this isn't always the case. Because not all situations are alike, sometimes we need unique types of protection magic for one thing or the other. I find that a multipronged approach should include general protection, personal protection, and the occasional specific protection. A home would require a different type of protection from, say, a child; and if that child were traveling on an airplane by themselves, that situation would require a specific type of protection.

In addition to what I list here, there are likely at least twenty objects in and around your home that can be used as an ally or tool in protection magic—in general, this would be anything that is black, sharp, pointy, causes irritation of some sort, or holds a particular image with meaning, like a shield or a sword. The glory of protection magic is that when push comes to shove, anything that can be used to harm you can also be used to protect you.

WORKING WITH THE MINERAL KINGDOM
in Protection Magic

Minerals and Gemstones: amber, amethyst, chrysocolla, diamond, emerald, hematite, jasper, jet, kyanite, labradorite, larimar, obsidian, onyx, peridot, prehnite, ruby, rutilated quartz, selenite, seraphinite, shungite, staurolite, smokey amethyst, smokey citrine, smokey quartz, sunstone, tiger's eye, tourmaline (especially black, green, and watermelon varieties), turquoise, tanzanite

Metals: bronze, iron, steel

Keep these stones on your person or wear in jewelry for personal protection. You can also put small tumbled stones over doorways and windows to hide protection magic in plain sight.

Of all the stones in the crystal kingdom that might lend their aid to our protection, black tourmaline is perhaps my favorite. In addition to assisting with our physical and mental security, it also protects us on a spiritual level. Any one of the stones listed above would make an excellent companion, however. Put a piece of tourmaline or tiger's eye in a bottle of glass cleaner and allow it to charge in the light of the full moon overnight. Use this empowered glass cleaner to clean windows and mirrors and ward them from negative influences.

Iron will protect you from magic and harmful spirits, especially the fae. Keep a piece on your altar to encourage safety in your workings. A blade from any of the metals listed here would be an excellent tool for protection magic.

Enchanting the steel used to create the frame or body of your vehicle for safety is another way of magically working with metal. To do this, put a circle of salt around your vehicle under the full moon and visualize the light from the moon collecting in the circle and then being absorbed by your vehicle. After a few moments, walk clockwise around your vehicle five times and chant, "Salt and earth, steel and might, strengthen metal with moonlight!" When you are finished, sweep the salt toward your car with a broom and chant, "Bless this (type of vehicle) and all it tows; keep them safe from harm and foes!"

WORKING WITH THE PLANT KINGDOM
in Protection Magic

Herbs and Trees: agrimony, alder, alkanet, angelica, anise, asafoetida, bamboo, barley, basil, bay, birch, blackberry, black pepper, black tea, boneset, broom, burdock, carnation, celandine, chamomile, cumin, damiana, devil pod, elder, eucalyptus, fern, feverfew, ginger, hawthorne, heather, henbane, holly, horehound, hyssop, Java citronella, lemon, lemongrass, lemon verbena, lime, mint, mistletoe, monkshood, mullein, nettle, pennyroyal, peony, primrose, rose, rosemary, rowan, rue, sage, slippery elm, Solomon's seal, thistle, valerian, violet, wormwood

Plant allies that have thorns are almost always associated with protection. Any botanical that has a pungent or unpleasant odor (such as asafoetida or valerian) can be used for protection as well. Truthfully, any plant that might make life unpleasant in any way can be used as a tool in warding magic, such as poison ivy, peppers, or nettles. The trick, of course, is handling these baneful plants with care so you do not fall victim to their effects.

A floor wash for protection can be made by brewing 1 ounce fresh stinging nettle with 1 cup boiling water. Allow it to steep for fifteen to twenty minutes and then combine with mop water to wash floors. As the stinging nettle steeps, the small needles will melt into the water, giving the water the properties of protection.

Rue is famous the world over for assisting in the protection of witches. Hang a sprig upside down on your front door to ward off evil and calamity or wear a piece in your hair when traveling to ensure a safe journey. It can be sprinkled in the shoes of children to keep them safe from harm.

For women seeking safety, working with heather is said to protect them from unwanted male advances and sexual violence. Heather mixed with red and white peppers and then powdered makes an effective dust that can be sprinkled near a sexual predator to banish them. A piece of valerian root tied together with a sprig of lavender and the thorny stem of a rose will make a powerful amulet against date rape. Wrap in a red cloth and carry in a purse.

LGBTQ+ witches will find strong plant allies for protection in Java citronella, damiana, devil pod, henbane, mint, monkshood, and lime. Plant Java citronella around the home and keep a piece in your pocket or purse to ward off STIs. A purple charm bag made on Thursday and stuffed with damiana, mint, and lime will ward off the attention of queerphobic people. Add monkshood seeds to ward off queerphobic hate crimes. An amulet made from a devil pod wrapped in red or black sinew under the new moon will provide safety at night when traveling alone.

Baneful plants—those
with thorns, unpleasant odors,
or that can make life difficult—
are great for protection magic in
general. Some are poisonous, so
make sure to do your research
before implementing
them in magic.

PROTECTION INCENSE

Burn over charcoal to imbue your workings with the power of protection or as a working all its own to encourage general protection of the home, family, and friends. Powder and then combine ½ ounce bay leaves, ½ ounce hyssop, ½ ounce rue, and ½ ounce dragon's blood resin.

Variations

Circle and Ritual: Add ⅓ ounce rose and ¼ ounce myrrh resin. Burn to assist in building boundaries between the worlds and for protection during a ritual. Make under the full moon, if possible, and store for later use.

For Safe Travel: Substitute rue with lemongrass and dragon's blood resin for frankincense resin. Pass through the smoke on the morning of a trip to ensure safe and smooth travel.

From Bad Luck and the Evil Eye: Add ⅓ ounce lemongrass and ⅓ ounce ground cloves. Burn near front door under the new moon to remove and protect against bad luck and the evil eye. Make on a Wednesday when the moon is waning.

From Corruption and Negative Influences: Add ½ ounce carnation and ⅓ ounce fern. Burn in the center of the home or where multiple people congregate. You can add this blend to 1 cup sea salt and place a line of this salt at the front and back doors once a month.

Energy Reversal: Add ⅓ ounce ginger and ½ ounce agrimony. Burn at dusk while facing the west and saying:

Go back, evil, from whence you came.
No more to bother me, no more to lame!
Return to the sender and leave me be
From your influence I am free!

> **Essential Oils:** basil, black pepper, camphor, clove, frankincense, galangal, geranium, heather, juniper, lemon, myrrh, palo santo, parsley, patchouli, pennyroyal, peppermint, pine, rue, sage, sandalwood, spearmint, vetiver

PROTECTION CONDITION OIL

In ½ ounce bottle, combine the following essential oils: 10 drops each black pepper and vetiver and 2 drops rue. Add a pinch of dried rue and galangal, then fill the rest of the bottle with a carrier oil and mix well.

Each full moon, dress any size black candle with this oil and dried nettle. As you light it, recite the following spell:

Spirits of the breathless moon
Be here now, not far or soon!
Follow me and watch my back
Guard me from evil attack!
Be by my side as I walk the way
Always attending both night and day.

Let the candle burn out on its own, over the course of several days if needed. Just be sure to have it totally burned down by the next full moon.

Variations

Sometimes there are specific conditions that require a small modification to the original recipe so that we can hone in on the right issues. Here are five other protection-type oils that you can make to help you do just that. Make these adjustments before adding carrier oil.

Against Bullying or Unwanted Attention: Add 3 drops frankincense essential oil and a pinch of dried comfrey leaves to the bottle. Dress shoes weekly on Sundays or prior to when you expect to see the bully.

Against Negative Spirits and Dark Entities: Substitute black pepper essential oil for clove essential oil and add 7 drops hyssop essential oil and a pinch of salt or iron shavings to the bottle. Lightly dress the top of your head and the bottom of your feet once a day with a single drop of oil each.

Against Physical and Sexual Abuse: Add 13 drops heather essential oil and, if possible, a few pieces of angelica root to the bottle. Write the suspected abuser's name on a 4x4" square of white paper with red ink, and then dress the center and four corners with the oil. Fold the paper three times in half, each time turning the paper counterclockwise and folding it away from you. Place this in your shoe when you are around them and replace it as needed. In addition to helping ward off their attention, it will also help to readjust the power dynamic between you and the abuser.

Against Corrupt Law Enforcement: Add a few pieces of Little John Chew (aka galangal) and 13 drops galangal essential oil. Once a week, dress the bottom of your shoes and the tires of your bike or car and recite the following charm:

Brickle brack and fiddy thorn
Safety to what you adorn.
Goodbye, PoPo, leave me be
I am not the one you see!

For Safe Travel: Add 7 drops mugwort oil. Dress any luggage and your chest with a single dab of oil before travel. Visualize a yellow protective aura forming around you and say, "From here to there and back again! So must it be!"

WORKING WITH COSMIC FORCES
in Protection Magic

> ***Houses and Signs:*** Aries, Cancer, Taurus
> ***Planets:*** Jupiter, Mars, Moon, Sun, Venus
> ***Days:*** Sunday, Monday, Tuesday, Thursday, Friday

When Mars, the moon, Jupiter, Venus, or the sun are transiting through one of these houses, magic for protection will be performed with ease. It is also a good time to do divination regarding ways in which you might need protection.

Perform powerful acts of protection on days ruled by these planets. On Sunday, when the sun is in rulership, protection magic regarding projects, groups, and your community can be performed with ease. On Mondays, when the moon rules, perform works of mental and emotional protection. On Tuesday, when Mars is in charge, perform reversal magic and install new wards and talismans for protection. On Thursday, when Jupiter rules, do magic to protect your home and belongings. Lastly, on Friday, while Venus reigns, perform magic to protect your finances and those you love.

WORKING WITH SPIRITS
in Protection Magic

Spirits: Ares, Bast, Brigid, St. Catherine, Diana, Freya, Freyr, Frigg, Ganesh, Green Tara, Hathor, Hera, Horus, Ishtar, Isis, St. Joseph, Kali, Lucifer, Lugh, Macha, Mars, Michael, Minerva, the Morrigan, Njord, Sekhmet, Thor, Venus, Vishnu

The spirits I have listed here are all known for being fierce protectors. Freya, Ganesh, Isis, Kali, and the Morrigan are known for being especially protective of children and the vulnerable. Diana protects women in labor. Hera, Ishtar, and Minerva are particularly protective of the home. Lucifer watches over those who are escaping religious persecution as well as those most vulnerable to religious attack. Ares, Sekhmet, the Morrigan, Michael, and Thor watch over members of the armed services while in battle.

Working with any of these spirits will be of benefit to your practice; however, it is always a good idea to get whatever spirits you are working with on board with your protection magic.

Draw this sigil and place it on your altar or in your Book of Shadows to encourage the spiritual forces in your life to work toward your protection.

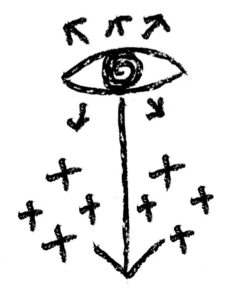

WORKING WITH SYMBOLS AND SYNCHRONICITY
in Protection Magic

> ***Tarot Cards:*** Emperor, Strength, Wheel of Fortune, Justice, Queen of Swords

There are actually several cards in the tarot that can be used for protection. In many ways, the tarot is a story told in seventy-eight parts, with each card representing something that might happen to us. To protect against what a card represents, place the card between two virgin mirrors (mirrors that no one has directly looked in) and leave it there until the potential danger has passed.

The Emperor card can be placed at the front door to help reassert boundaries that someone may be crossing. The Justice and Queen of Swords cards can be placed under a doormat to protect those who live in the home from gossip. The Strength card can be placed in a bookbag or purse to protect women from harm, and the Wheel of Fortune card can be placed in a Book of Shadows to help keep it safe from prying eyes.

> ***Iconography:*** axe, castle, Celtic shield knot, equal-armed cross, evil eye, eye of Horus, hammer, hamsa, Hecate's wheel, helm of awe, hexagram, mirror, pentagram, shield, triskelle, triquetra

Each of these symbols makes for an excellent companion in your protection magic. Mirrors are often used to reflect energy back to their sender, and they make excellent additions to the sides of the home or property to protect against nosy neighbors. Placing the symbol of a hamsa hand or evil eye over your door is known to ward off jealousy and spite. A hexagram will protect you from harm caused by spirits, and the axe will cut through spells that may have been sent your way. Draw the wheel of Hecate in chalk on the ground to keep yourself safe while astral traveling.

HAMSA

HECATE'S WHEEL

TRISKELLE

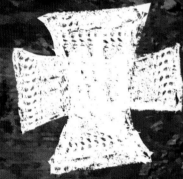

EQUAL-ARMED CROSS

HELM OF AWE

HAMMER

AXE

CASTLE

CELTIC SHIELD KNOT

Protection icons

HEXAGRAM

EVIL EYE

PENTAGRAM

SHIELD

MIRROR

EYE OF HORUS

TRIQUETRA

Animals and Insects: ant, badger, bear, bee, blue jay, boar, crab, crow, dog, eel, horse, hornet/ wasp, jackal, lion, octopus, owl, peacock, porcupine, shark, stag, tiger, toad, wolf

The animal kingdom is full of protective forces that can assist our magic. When working with animal remains, teeth and claws are usually preferred. The majority of the animals listed here are endangered and their remains would be incredibly hard to come by. These are best engaged symbolically or shamanically. There is, however, a long-standing tradition of working with animal remains in protection magic. Easy to obtain and cruelty-free, shark teeth are frequently shed and sold all over as a novelty. Porcupine quills can be procured, which are also shed. On the other hand, chicken feet, especially those from a rooster containing spurs, are often preserved and used in the making of protection talismans.

Colors: black, brown, gold, purple, red, silver, white

Pet collars should be made of the colors listed here and empowered on your altar under the full moon. Fit them with a silver charm to gain the favor and protection of the Witch Queen. Of all colors, black is known to be the most protective, and the majority of witches, including myself, tend to have a lot of it in our wardrobes for this reason. It absorbs all light and negative energy, and when worn it acts as a sort of spiritual and psychic armor. Tie a black ribbon around anything you want protected and incorporate it into your working for protection.

Numbers: 2, 3, 5, 9, 11

The numbers listed here are awfully potent on their own. Make two charm bags for protection and place them on either side of the front door of your home to keep all who enter safe. A simple charm bag recipe might include nine pinches each of rue, salt, and black pepper, bound together in a black cloth with a red or silver string.

CHAPTER FIVE

Burn nine brown candles in a court-case working to ensure protection from corrupt law enforcement. Place three pieces of moonstone under your bed to protect yourself from nightmares and sleep paralysis. Keep five pennies in your pocket at all times to draw money. Place eleven flowers in a vase and place it on your altar to draw opportunities for financial growth.

BLACK SALT

Salt, in general, can be used for cleansing and protection, but black salt takes the properties of regular salt to the next level. In occultism we have worked with black salt for longer than anyone can trace, but its use is mostly seen today in modern Conjure as well as Hoodoo and Santeria. To be clear, we are not talking about the expensive culinary salt that you can buy from fancy foodie stores. It is likely that if you ate this black salt, you would become ill, so ingestion should be avoided at all costs.

Used for protection, banishment, and curse removal, black salt can be worked with as a spell on its own or as a component in spells. It can be lightly sprinkled around the parameter, in the cardinal corners (those closest to north, south, east, and west), across the threshold of the front and back doors, or at the beginning of a driveway to protect the home.

There are many different recipes for black salt, all of which involve mixing regular salt (preferably sea salt) with ashes or soot of some kind. The earliest recipes I have been able to find instruct the practitioner to scrape the smoky carbon deposit from the inside of an oil lamp. This substance is known as "lamp black"; however, similar natural carbon deposits can be collected and used to make black salt, such as "furnace black" or "cauldron black."

Some recipes call for mixing salt with ashes from the nine sacred trees. The list of what exactly those trees are, however, varies from location to location. The most common list appears to be ash, birch, elm, oak, hawthorn, hazel, yew, and willow.

Traditionally, dyes were not used in the making of black salt, but it is a frequent occurrence to see these days. Natural inks from cuttlefish, squid, and octopi or even ink from a pen or stamp pad can be used. Acrylic and watercolor paints also can be added to increase the color intensity.

To make our black salt, however, we will be working with a combination of all these techniques. After years of trial and error, not to mention failed attempts at procuring hard-to-find ingredients required for more classic recipes, I came up with a few of my own. This one will do a phenomenal job and is simple to make.

What You Will Need

- small sage smudge bundle
- a firesafe dish
- ⅓ cup activated charcoal powder
- 6 tablespooons water
- 2 cups sea salt
- mixing bowls
- baking sheet

Part One: Prepare the Ashes

Burn the sage bundle and use the fire-safe dish to collect the ash. While it burns, use this time to smudge your home, self, and anything else you can think of. Part of what makes this ash so magical to use is that it was made in the process of cleansing.

Once you have burned at least two-thirds of the sage, put the smudge out by dabbing the bundle like a cigar in the fire-safe dish until it goes out. If you find this process difficult to do, dunk the bundle in water to extinguish. Discard remaining sage, if any.

Once cooled, combine all of the ashes from the bundle and place them in a mixing bowl. Some of this may be chunky; that is okay as long as the chunks aren't too much bigger than the salt. Pulverize them with the flat side of a spoon to break them apart if needed.

By ash of sage
and sacred fire
This black salt
is my desire

Part Two: Making the Salt

Add activated charcoal powder to your ashes and combine. After this is mixed well, add the 6 tablespooons of water and blend this mixture into a slightly runny paste about the consistency of acrylic paint. Add more water if needed to achieve this. Add the salt and combine until ingredients are mixed well. Evenly spread the salt mixture on the baking sheet.

Using your index finger, draw a pentagram or other protection symbol into the salt. Say, "By ash of sage and sacred fire, this black salt is my desire. Break all curses and all evil; save the worthy from upheaval. Remove the bad and keep the good; let nothing stand where you have stood. With these words I cast this spell: let power surge and magic swell. This black salt shall set us free; by the sun so must it be!"

Set baking sheet in the sun to dry for twenty-four to forty-eight hours. Once dry, collect and store for later use.

THE WITCH'S FOOT

The witch's foot is an original spell by yours truly designed to ward off harmful spells and unwelcome spirits. When made properly, the witch's foot will keep the person who possesses it, as well as all those in the home, from falling victim to these influences. A type of charm bag, hang the witch's foot over the fireplace, at the point of intersection between rooms, on the front door, or, if needed, hide it.

What You Will Need

- a small black cloth bag with tie
- needle and white thread or white paint and small paintbrush
- the witch's foot symbol (see image on bag, right)
- 3-inch circle of parchment paper
- black ink pen
- protection condition oil (any blend for protection will work)
- 5 pinches white copal, divided
- protection incense
- 5 pieces of thorny rose stem
- rue
- cat's claw bark
- five-finger grass
- magnetic sand (also known as "iron shavings," this metal sand is used for attraction and is sometimes called "lodestone food," as it is often sold with lodestones)
- 3–5 shark teeth
- Florida water (rue water works quite nicely, as does any alcohol that evaporates quickly, like whiskey or rum)

The tracks I lay
are not to follow

Making the Witch's Foot

First things first: cleanse the black bag by passing it through protection incense three times, then sew or paint the witch's foot pattern onto one side. Do this in an X or cross-stitch pattern if sewing, and while doing so, chant:

> *Untouched by blade or arrow*
> *The witch's path crook and narrow.*
> *The tracks I lay are not to follow*
> *All threats of evil now made hollow.*
> *When something bad comes knocking about*
> *What lies within shall grow a snout.*
> *And from that snout shall grow sharp teeth*
> *Capturing it and dragging it beneath.*

After you finish painting or stitching the sigil onto the bag, go ahead and draw the sigil on the circle of parchment. Write your name over the sigil three times.

Turn the circle clockwise 90 degrees and then write the words "protect, defend, serve" three times over your name.

Anoint the center of the paper three times with protection condition oil using your finger.

Fold the circle in half toward you, rotate it clockwise another 90 degrees, then repeat this two more times so that the paper has been folded three times. Once you have done this, place a tiny piece of copal inside the folds and set aside.

Light your incense and pass the bag over it five times while chanting, "By black and thin, we now begin."

Open the bag, take a deep breath, and then exhale fully into it as if your breath was the breath of life it needs to come alive. Visualize a white spark leaving your body, entering the bag, being absorbed into the cloth, and making the sigil of the witch's foot on the front of the bag glow like a white flame.

Assemble the bag by stuffing it with alternating layers of the herbs until it is half full.

Take the folded parchment in your passive hand (the one you don't write with) and say:

> *Protect, defend, serve me and only me as your master.*
> *Protect, defend, serve me with the force of a Titan.*
> *Protect, defend, serve me until I release you from this bond!*

Then place it in the bag along with the shark teeth and magnetic sand. Fill the rest of the bag up with alternating layers of herbs and then tie the top of the bag tightly with a triple knot.

Take the freshly constructed amulet in your hands and look deeply into the sigil of the witch's foot. Say:

> *Untouched by blade or arrow*
> *The witch's path, crooked and narrow.*
> *The tracks I lay are not to follow*
> *All threats of evil forever hollow.*
> *When bad comes knocking about*
> *Come alive and show thy snout.*
> *And in that snout shall be sharp teeth*
> *To capture it and drag it beneath.*
> *O witch's foot, I conjure thee:*
> *Protect, defend, serve only me!*

Lastly, "feed" it Florida water (or substitute) by placing it in a tiny dish and allowing to soak for two hours. The alcohol should evaporate rapidly, but after two hours take it out of the bath and let it dry completely. Once a month, under the full moon, "feed" it Florida water (or substitute) by following this same process. Again, dry completely before hanging it up.

Your witch's foot should remain active as long as it is fed. Depending on how much energy it is taking on for you, you should only need to replace it when it becomes old and starts falling apart. I tend to remake mine once a year or so, just to keep things fresh.

THE "BOTTLE OF 1,000 EYES" SPELL

Okay, so this may sound a bit extra, but this spell really does employ the use of hundreds of tiny eyes—black-eyed peas behaving as eyes on your behalf, to be exact. This is a type of bottle spell, and while there probably aren't going to be a thousand black-eyed peas in your jar, the poetry sure is nice.

For this working, all you need is a bottle (I used an empty wine bottle), enough black-eyed peas to fill the bottle three-fourths of the way up, about an ounce (or more if desired) of protection condition oil, and enough corn oil to fill the bottle the rest of the way to the top. The dried black-eyed peas each represent a tiny little eye that is looking out for you. Do not used freshly harvested or cooked black-eyed peas. Corn oil is used in this working because it comes from a plant whose fruit is called an "ear," lending the ability to listen out for you as well.

Once you have made your bottle, say:

> *Eyes to watch my back*
> *Ears to listen for attack!*
> *Assembled here as a ward—*
> *Against silver tongue and the sword!*

Place the bottle somewhere high and refill with oil as needed. If the bottle becomes discolored or something happens to it, like it falls off a shelf and breaks, this means trouble is coming!

Black-eyed peas act as eyes in this bottle spell.

HEXENSPIEGEL

The hexenspiegel is a German folk charm that is used to protect the home or property from acts of bewitchment and the evil eye, as well as from baneful spirits. A smaller version can be made and worn as an amulet. Traditionally, these are made from pieces of broken mirror, which are said to be bad luck to anyone who might gaze into them. The pieces are carefully collected and then made into these charms under the dark or new moon. Once they have been constructed, they can be hung anywhere as active wards.

Hexenspiegels are famous sentinels known for being among some of the most powerful amulets a witch can use for protection. While I cannot recommend you go playing with broken glass, I can offer you a safer alternative that will still get the job done. This will require a special trip to the craft store to purchase a small craft mirror (round or square) that is at least one inch wide (the bigger, the better), as well as polymer or self-drying clay. While it is optional for this spell, I find adding crystals and other curios such as shark teeth, porcupine quills, or even iron nails can benefit the working and give the hexenspiegel a personality all its own. Be careful, however, since we will want the sharp end of these things pointing out. Do not hurt yourself or put the end product where someone could get hurt. Again, make wise choices.

What You Will Need

- protection incense
- craft mirror
- polymer or self-drying clay
- knife or sculpting tool
- black permanent marker
- open-eye pin (also known as "bead landing eye pins") or bendable craft wire
- glue
- pointy curios (optional)
- black acrylic paint and brush

*Use any pointy curios
you might have available,
such as crystals, shark
teeth, porcupine quills,
or iron nails.*

Part One: Preparing the Mirror and Clay

Light the protection incense and then cleanse and empower a palm-sized piece of clay and the craft mirror by passing them through the smoke three times each.

Roll the chunk of clay into a smooth ball and then flatten it to the same thickness as the mirror.

Place the mirror in the center of the clay (do not push down) and then use a knife or sculpting tool to remove all clay that extends past one inch from the edge of the mirror. Once you have done this, remove the mirror and place extra clay off to the side; you'll need it in part three.

On the back of the mirror, draw a pentagram with the black permanent marker and let dry.

Glue the bottom of the eye pin to the back of the mirror so that the "eye," or hook, extends about ½ inch from the edge of the mirror. Alternatively, bend the wire to make a hook and glue it to the back side of the mirror. Let dry.

Part Two: Construction

Once the glue has dried, position the mirror at the center of the clay so that the reflective side is facing away from the clay.

Gently roll the edge of the clay inward and then mold it to the outer edges of the mirror to create a protective barrier around the glass. You will need to mold the clay around the open eye pin or wire. Smooth out edges and gently press the clay into the back of the mirror.

Part Three: Optional Embellishment

Using your extra clay and pointy curios, be creative and add additional features to your hexenspiegel. Mold the clay around the objects to bring firmness and support, and attach them to the outer edges of the mirror. Be sure not to weigh it down too much with extra material, as that could cause issues during drying as well as affect how well the final product is able to hang on its own.

Part Four: Finish Construction and Empowerment

Bake or dry clay as instructed by product maker.

Blessed be the witch's mirror

Once dry and firm, paint the clay black to cover any original neutral color. Feel free to be creative and add other colors to this, especially gold, red, or white; just keep the base black. Add texture, protection symbols, and other embellishments to incorporate as much magic into the amulet as possible. Allow to dry when finished.

At dusk, go outside with the hexenspiegel and catch the reflection of the setting sun over your shoulder in the mirror. Say:

> *Blessed be the witch's mirror, many are its ways.*
> *Blessed be the witch's mirror, catching the last rays.*
> *Blessed be those it watches, many are at play.*
> *Blessed be those it watches, keeping harm at bay.*

Once the hexenspiegel has been empowered, you are free to hang it anywhere! Cleanse and recharge once a month under the new moon by passing it through protection incense smoke and reciting the incantation from the empowerment above.

THE GOLEM FETISH

A golem is an earthen figure made from clay that resembles the shape of a human and is ensorcelled to become the body of a disembodied spirit. Golems can range in size from small figurines to that of a full-sized person. The spirits that possess golems are generally service-oriented, meaning they come to assist the practitioner in his or her magical tasks. Depending on the culture you come from, the creation of a golem might be known to you as one of the very first acts of magic ever performed. In Abrahamic mythology, the first man, known as Adam, was made by molding clay.

Golems are said to be powerful and can take on a life of their own. In the story of the Golem of Prague, a rabbi creates a life-size golem to protect the Jewish citizens of Prague who had been ordered to be put to death by the Holy Roman Emperor, Rudolph II. Turning to mysticism and the occult, Rabbi Bezalel created the golem from clay found on the banks of a nearby river and then enchanted it to come alive through ritual. The golem protected Jewish citizens until it began to develop needs and urges of its own. In some versions of the story, the golem falls in love with a young woman; in others, it turns on the rabbi and tries to kill him and his congregation.

In modern popular mythology, Princess Diana of Themyscira, also known as Wonder Woman, shares a similar origin. Her mother, longing for a child, formed the shape of a baby from clay. To her surprise, the goddess Aphrodite appeared and brought the clay figure to life in the form of a newborn girl.

Golems require specific instruction and purpose for them to work, regardless of size. They will execute your orders exactly as given, so before you construct one, think carefully about what you will want it to do. What I really like about working with golems is that they are excellent tools to work with when protecting people or places that you can't always see to keep an eye on, such as children, your home, or even yourself! Our golem will be a figurine-sized guardian that will be given the specific task of protecting a family.

Note: It is preferable to use self-drying clay, pottery clay, or mud for this working. Polymer clay will work in a pinch, but the synthetic nature of the polymer is believed to cause problems for the golem long-term.

What You Will Need

- red ink pen
- 3 x 3-inch square of parchment paper
- protection incense (not pictured)
- red string
- ½ pound of clay
- sculpting tools (not pictured)
- 1 or 2 small protection stones (see list at the beginning of the chapter)
- nail or similarly sized stick that has been sharpened on one end to a point
- 4 small black candles (not pictured)

Part One: Drafting Your Commands and Sculpting the Golem

Using the red ink pen, write three command instructions for the golem to follow once it is activated. These should be simple and direct, such as "1: Protect me and my family from evil and harm. 2: Protect our home from evil and harm. 3: Protect our vehicles from evil and harm." Or "1: Protect me from physical harm at all times. 2: Protect me from malicious witchcraft at all times. 3: Protect me from negative spirits at all times."

Under the three commands, write "As I order it, so shall it be" and sign your name.

Light the protection incense and pass the parchment through the smoke to empower it. Tightly roll the parchment into a scroll and tie a piece of red string around it.

Divide your clay into two equal pieces and set one aside. Divide the remaining clay into five equal pieces and set aside.

Using your sculpting tools, take the largest piece of clay and remove a chunk of clay large enough for the scroll to fit into it. This is the body of your golem. Place the scroll inside of the cavity and then use the removed clay to fill in the hole (see inset photo above). Smooth out any roughness with your fingers.

Next, take two of the smaller pieces and roll them into legs, then attach to the bottom of the body. Smooth out where they were joined and flatten the bottoms of the feet so it can stand.

Using two more pieces of clay, form the shoulders, arms, and hands of the figure. Join the hands together at the center of the torso.

Using the final piece of clay, mold a head for this figure. Use the two small protection stones as eyes. Attach head to rest of body. Smooth out where the pieces were joined.

Take a few moments and use your creativity to adjust the form and add features if you like.

Part Two: Empower the Golem

Take the nail or sharp stick and pass it through the incense smoke ten times. Each time, chant:

> *A tool to protect, a tool to maim.*
> *A tool to defend, a tool with great aim!*

Plunge the nail or stick into the hands of the figure and mold the clay around it. Allow drying. On the next full moon, light the protection incense again and place the golem in the center of four black candles.

Light the candles. Say:

> *Shaped from earth and empowered by the moon*
> *Bearing the mark of the sacred rune.*
> *Golem, awaken and hear my voice*
> *To obey my orders you have no choice!*
> *Serve as I command, this vessel fill*
> *You are a creature brought forth by will!*

Let the candles go out on their own. Once they do, your golem is alive! Keep it alive by feeding it every full moon and making offerings of alcohol, incense, or tobacco. Place your golem on your altar or somewhere safe where it will remain undisturbed.

When you no longer desire your golem's assistance, break him in half and take out the scroll. Remove the nail, then bury the remains.

Keep your golem
alive by feeding it every
full moon and making
offerings of alcohol,
incense, or tobacco.

Chapter 6
PROSPERITY MAGIC

Money. We all need it, and we all want it. This is not our fault; we live in a capitalistic society that uses money to trade everything in the realm of goods and services, and everything from the price of gas to the cost of food is based on what is going on with the global economy. Whether we like it or not, this is our reality, and it doesn't have to be fair for it to be true. For us to live in this world, we need money, and we need more of it than just enough to get by.

Money is a form of power in this imbalanced culture of ours. If you have enough of it, the world is your oyster and you can literally get away with murder. If you don't have any money at all and find yourself homeless, then you quickly learn that you have almost no power in the human world, relying on the kindness of spirits and strangers just to make it through the week. If you are a woman, you are likely to get paid less than your male counterparts because of some archaic belief that you should be at home in the kitchen instead of in the workplace. If you are a person of color, you are less likely to get higher-paying jobs or even the education needed for those higher-paying jobs because of the same archaic system. The system might work, but it only works well for a few of us, and even then just enough for the majority to stay focused on the carrot. The system, however, has its victims too, and for the top 10 percent to exist, the remaining 90 percent, especially that 30 percent at the bottom, has to survive as well.

Money magic is born from the struggle to exist in this system. You won't find a lot of spells or rituals to make one a millionaire, but you will find a rich and diverse history of spells to help people make the most of the system and even beat it at its own game.

GET YOUR MIND ON YOUR MONEY

Money used to scare the hell out of me—to be honest, it still makes me sweat a little. I come from the middle of nowhere. My parents don't have a lot of money, and as a kid, it was all about growing our own food, hunting, and saving as much as possible. While I can appreciate the education in self-preservation that lifestyle provided us, it was out of absolute necessity. My parents are good, hardworking folks. They taught me how to work hard in return, but they didn't ever teach me how to manage money.

I spent years living paycheck to paycheck, and I wasn't always able to make it work. There were short-term spells that worked great, but they never actually solved my problem. I worked extra jobs and found I was able to make extra cash, but I never seemed to have it when I needed it. Eventually, I found myself turning twenty-eight and realized that every time I looked out at my future, my financial situation was unclear—and not only was it unclear, but it was causing me to get very anxious and feel powerless. Over the years—between student loans, cars, and credit cards—I had racked up quite a lot of debt and was desperately needing a new way of approaching the matter. Feeling powerless definitely wasn't working, and quick money spells weren't going to get me out of debt.

I swallowed my fear and went back to school for accounting. The goal wasn't to become an accountant; it was to get a better understanding of what I was so scared of. What I learned there totally changed my approach to how I dealt with my money and how I approached my money magic. Everything I thought I knew and just about everything I had been taught was wrong.

THE THREE THINGS YOU NEED TO DO INSTANTLY

As you will notice, these all have to do with switching your perspective regarding your personal relationship to money. We could do all the money magic in the world, but if your personal relationship to finances is toxic or working against you, then nothing will actually help you long-term. Doing these things helps you find the power in finances and take your power back from past financial shortcomings.

Lose the pagan poverty mindset. If there was one money spell I wish I could whip up, it would be that I got a dollar for every time I heard a spiritual or pagan person say, "Pagans aren't known for being wealthy" or "I'm spiritual, so I don't need money; I have my work." By saying that the spiritually inclined aren't known for having money, you are putting a significant cap on the potential of magic, specifically your magic. Also, I happen to know more than a few millionaire witches myself, and I don't think I have ever heard them buy into something so self-sabotaging. I know I keep saying it, but magic follows the path of least resistance, and all you are doing by subscribing to this mindset is creating a well-worn psychic path for poverty.

Being poor doesn't make you more spiritual; that is a false equivalent. The history of spirituality is full of people who gave up their wealth to become spiritual or more connected, like the Buddha. What people often forget, though, is that the Buddha was rich before he was poor. For him, giving up wealth was a sacrifice and an act of stepping into a more intense spiritual state. If you are like me and grew up poor or you never had any wealth to give up to begin with, then being poor doesn't add to your spiritual state in the way it did for the Buddha. For you, the work of spirituality may very well be that you work to get yourself out of poverty or from that tight financial situation. You aren't a monk, you aren't a nun, you aren't the Buddha; you are someone who has to pay bills and taxes.

Your gods and the spirits you work with want you to be successful. If you aren't stressed out all the time and are actually able to focus on your spirituality, then they get what *they* want and you get what *you* want. If you work with spirits that *don't* want success for you, I invite you to take a look at why you are working with them to begin with.

Stop being afraid of your money; ignorance is not bliss. How do you know if you are afraid of your money? You avoid looking at your bank statements and your account balances. This was a big one for me. I really hated checking my account and would do just about anything to avoid knowing what was actually in the account. Knowing was almost worse than not knowing, and just keeping a tab in my head somehow gave me a sense of false security. By doing a simple Google search, I found that I was not alone. There are millions of people who are in the same boat, and we are sabotaging ourselves every day.

To take power over our finances and our money juju, we have to seek total clarity over financial matters, and we have to take ownership of our financial responsibilities. We also must be able to look the devil right in the eyes and not be the one to blink first. I made a habit of checking my bank account every morning over coffee and starting off my day with total awareness. Not only did this help me get control over my accounts, but it helped me plan. This became part of a ritual I would do in the name of the goddess Fortuna, who we will talk about more in just a bit. Taking my power back from my financial demon meant that it suddenly had less power and I could defeat it.

In doing this, a few major shifts happened almost immediately. I noticed that when I wasn't afraid of my money, my money wasn't afraid to accumulate and stick around. Several spirits are associated with money, and they got a lot friendlier when I was no longer avoiding them.

Don't treat money like it's a force of nature; *you're* the force of nature. Money has a lot of power, but it is something invented by humans, which means it is just as vulnerable as humans. When funds aren't available, don't let it make you feel defeated; the war is not over! If you find yourself in a financial bind, sit down and trace your financial steps, look for where you could have adjusted, and then make a plan for how to avoid making that mistake in the future. If there is no money at all and no way of getting any, then you need to reach out for help and be direct with any agency or persons you owe money to. Statistically speaking, most people who fall behind or can't keep up on payments do not take advantage of programs and services that could help them avoid a lot of unnecessary fees and drama. While you can do magic to gain the favor of the institutions you owe, reaching out is always the first step.

WORKING WITH THE MINERAL KINGDOM
in Prosperity Magic

> **Minerals and Gemstones:** agate (especially moss and fire varieties), amber, aventurine, calcite (especially yellow and orange varieties), citrine, clear quartz, garnet, green tourmaline, jade, jasper (especially yellow, green, and ocean varieties), lodestone, malachite, opal, peridot, pyrite, sapphire, sunstone, tiger's eye, topaz
> **Metals:** copper, gold, nickel

The mineral kingdom is full of stones that are known for helping with prosperity, but there are a few that stick out as time-tested favorites. Citrine is a variety of quartz that often possesses a gold, orange, or green hue. One of its names is "merchant stone" because it is known for being used by those in retail to increase the flow of commerce. Putting a piece together with pyrite in a cash box will increase cash sales. Wearing citrine or having it on your person will also assist you in making better financial decisions and help you get the best deal during the loan process.

Pyrite can take
the place of gold
in most spells.

Jade is seen in the East, primarily China, as a symbol of wealth and prosperity as well as good fortune. It is often given as a gift at marriages, births, and other important life events. Carry a piece of jade with you when you want to attract independent income or extra cash. Charge the jade on your altar and carry it with you if you gamble or do any betting.

Pyrite, or fool's gold, looks like gold but isn't metal and therefore cannot be refined into something of similar value. It can, however, take the place of gold in most spells. Add it to prosperity charm bags to increase the gravity of the working. Carry a piece of pyrite with you at work to attract a promotion or raise.

Both moss and fire agates can be worn or carried by people in the food service industry to attract and protect tips and gratuity. Ocean jasper works similarly. In addition to attracting tips and other like income, it is ideal for assisting those who are saving their money or paying off loan debt. These three stones are also excellent to work with when someone owes you money and you want to be paid back ASAP.

Work with sapphire to aid in paying off student loans, opal when you want to take out a loan, and peridot when you want to renegotiate the terms of a loan.

Amber, garnet, and sapphire will assist you in setting up new accounts, trusts, funds, and other financial profiles. These stones are also excellent for assisting in the investment process and helping to find good stocks.

Lodestones are naturally energized magnetite that are often used in magic to attract things. Generally, we find them used most often in work related to drawing money in. To work with a lodestone, name it and place it over a piece of paper that has your name written on it three times before giving it a place to live prominently in the home. "Feed" the lodestone once a week by sprinkling magnetic sand, iron shavings, and Florida water on it.

Gold should be worn to attract prosperity and is easily charged in the sunlight. When added to prosperity spell work, it lends the power of the sun to your workings.

To tap into the flow of wealth moving through the economy, paint the head side of a penny or nickel red and then spend it. As it circulates, it will draw prosperity back to you.

WORKING WITH THE PLANT KINGDOM
in Prosperity Magic

Plants, Herbs, and Trees: alfalfa, alkanet, allspice, almond, apple, bamboo, basil, beans (any kind), beech, bergamot, birch, black tea, calendula, cedar, chamomile, chestnut, cinnamon, clove, clover, comfrey, devil's shoestring, dill, dragon's blood, elder, fenugreek, fern, frankincense, geranium, High John root, honeysuckle, Irish moss, lucky hand root, maple, mesquite, oak, oats, orange, palm, parsley, patchouli, pine, pomegranate, rose of Jericho, sassafras, skullcap, snapdragon, Spanish moss, thyme, tomato, tulip, valerian, vanilla bean, vetiver

Plant allies that have abundant seeds, fruit, seed pods in the shape of coins, or leaves in the shape of coins are almost always associated with prosperity, as well as anything that has a sweet scent. Each one of the plants listed here would help make a useful ally, but there are a few that stick out.

Work with bamboo, beans, clover, mint, and tomato to assist in spells and other workings for fast cash. These fast-growing plants have a high yield and easy turnover, so the workings will also be limited in their scope. After picking a tomato, rub paper money with your hands and put it in your purse or wallet to attract hidden or unknown sources of income.

Spanish moss and other like mosses are commonly used for stuffing dolls and charm bags to create opportunities for making money or increasing trade. Hanging Spanish moss over your front door is said to bring fortune and increase the sale of goods.

To attract a new job or financial opportunity, place a dried rose of Jericho in a bowl of spring or distilled water and watch it unfold. After five days, remove the plant and allow it to dry back up. Save the remaining water and dump it onto your front porch or wipe down your front door with it under the full moon.

For gambling, wrap the money you will use with a fresh comfrey leaf that has been dressed with prosperity oil, then place this in your wallet for three days. After the third day, the money will be charged with gambling luck and whatever you spend will come back at least threefold.

Work with sassafras for business matters, especially when it comes to finances and protecting them. Put a piece over the front door of your business to encourage foot traffic. Make a tea from sassafras and use it as a floor wash at the entrance to the business. Place a piece of sassafras with five pieces of clove and place them in the register to keep it protected. To ward off bad financial entanglements and investments, keep a green charm bag stuffed with sassafras, clove, patchouli, and mint on your business altar.

PROSPERITY INCENSE

Burn over charcoal to imbue your workings with prosperity or as a working of its own to encourage general prosperity and financial growth. Powder and then combine ⅓ ounce patchouli, ¼ teaspoon cinnamon, ⅓ ounce sassafras, and ½ ounce dragon's blood.

Variations

To Attract Steady Income: Add ½ ounce amber resin. Blend under the full moon. Burn every Friday and whenever doing any career planning.

To Attract New Income: Substitute cinnamon with sweetgrass. Add ⅓ ounce amber resin. Burn in the front of the home or near the hearth on Fridays.

For Credit-Related Matters and Debt Recovery: Omit all spice. Substitute copal resin for dragon's blood. Add ⅓ ounce mint. Blend under the new moon. Burn at dusk or when working with creditors.

For Accounting and Working with the IRS: Substitute honeysuckle for patchouli and frankincense for dragon's blood. Blend under the full moon and burn on Thursday and Friday mornings as well as before meetings with an accountant or IRS professional.

To Compel Payment: Substitute cinnamon with clove. Add ⅓ ounce thyme and ⅓ ounce frankincense. Burn on Wednesdays and Fridays to compel a debtor to pay you back.

Money, money,
come to me
In no one's debt
I'll ever be!

> *Essential Oils:* ambergris, apple blossom, basil, bergamot, blood orange, cinnamon, frankincense, ginger, heliotrope, honeysuckle, lemon balm, lily of the valley, mint, nutmeg, oak moss, patchouli, tonka, vanilla, vetiver

PROSPERITY CONDITION OIL

Put 1½ teaspoons chipped cinnamon bark in a ½ ounce bottle and combine the following essential oils: 7 drops frankincense, 7 drops vetiver, and 7 drops amber. Fill the rest of the bottle with a carrier oil and mix well.

To empower the oil, place the bottle on your altar at the center of a circle made from pyrite (or another prosperity stone) under the waxing moon. Let it remain there for seven days. Each day gently shake the bottle. After the seventh day, the oil is ready to use!

Variations

Sometimes there are specific conditions that require a small modification to the original recipe so that we can hone in on the right issues. Here are five other prosperity oils to help you do just that. Make these adjustments before adding carrier oil.

Fast Cash: Add 13 drops peppermint essential oil and a pinch of magnetic sand. Excellent to wear when working in the service industry to attract tips. May also be used for gambling or to attract opportunities for fast cash. Add a small chunk of pyrite to skip the empowerment process and use right way.

Responsible Money Management: Add 7 drops galangal essential oil. Omit cinnamon bark. Rub one drop on your palm and then rub with both hands. Gently dress a bank deposit slip by rubbing your hands on it. Diffuse only the essential oil blend when balancing checkbooks and on Friday mornings.

Block Buster / Big Break: Add a pinch of chamomile flowers to the bottle in addition to the cinnamon. Add 7 drops blood orange essential oil and 7 drops dragon's blood essential oil. Instead of pyrite, use five pieces of citrine to charge the oil.

Loan Buster: Substitute amber essential oil with honeysuckle essential oil. Wear when meeting with loan officers or paying off loans. Diffuse only the essential oil blend on Mondays and Wednesdays to help clear a path to relieve loan debt.

Attract Large Wealth: Triple the strength of the oil by adding 21 drops each of the original oils. To this add 21 drops dragon's blood essential oil. Empower the oil within a circle of seven different prosperity stones.

WORKING WITH COSMIC FORCES
in Prosperity Magic

Houses and Signs: Capricorn, Leo, Virgo
Planets: Jupiter, Venus
Days: Thursday, Friday

When Jupiter or Venus are transiting through Capricorn, Leo, or Virgo, they will aid any act of magic devoted to prosperity. During these times it is also a good idea to perform divination that is geared toward long-term understanding of financial growth, goal setting, and family planning.

Thursdays are excellent times to perform works related to growth and business planning. On Fridays, when Venus has a dominant influence, magic related to immediate income and commerce is best performed.

JUPITER BUDGET WORKING

The first thing you need to do is set some goals for your future financial outlook. Come up with at least five unique challenges to set for yourself, such as to pay off student loans, be free of credit card debt, pay off your car early, be on time with bill payments, open a business one day, or go

Your gods and the spirits
you work with want you
to be successful

Money doesn't grow
on trees, nor does it manifest
overnight. Generally speaking,
money magic tends to be a slow burn
and requires a solid plan of action
for how you are going to be open to
receiving new streams of income.
Nothing beats having a
long-term plan!

on vacation. Now turn those goals into positive, affirmative proclamations that suggest these things are already happening and true. To pay off student loans becomes "All of my student loans are fully paid," to be on time with bill payments becomes "All of my bills have been paid on time," and so on.

Next, you need to make a budget. Yes, it sucks, and they are boring, and magic should be all candles and incense and stuff, but make one anyway! Include all of your income and monthly expenses, and while you are doing that, go ahead and put the due dates for your bills and other expenses on a calendar. Take a few moments and think about what it is going to take for those bills to get paid on time for the following month. Next, take a few moments and ask yourself one earnest question: How much money can you save each month?

This can be anything that is realistic for you and your personal situation, but you will need to save something, even if it is only a dusty penny from under the couch cushion. For me, money flows a bit differently than the average person because my work is primarily as a medium and professional witch, and streams of income are usually seasonal. In the case where your income might be seasonal, project-based, or maybe you work in the service industry, where tips and revenue are intermittent, you might want to consider deciding on a certain percentage of income to save per check or shift to make it a bit easier.

Once you have those things figured out, take a piece of parchment paper and draw the Seal of Jupiter (see opposite page) in the middle of the paper so that it is roughly similar in size to what you see here. Use black ink. On the top half of the paper, write out your budget; on the bottom half, write out your five proclamations. On the day of the working (which should be a Thursday), read aloud the entire contents of the page and bless this paper with prosperity condition oil. Stare intensely into the Seal of Jupiter at the center, recite your affirmative proclamations three more times, and draw upon the power of Jupiter by saying, "Jupiter expanding, Jupiter flow, Jupiter rising, make this so!"

Store it somewhere safe where it can be referenced weekly, such as your Book of Shadows. Each Thursday revisit this parchment and read over it again. Be sure to read aloud its entire contents and to speak aloud your proclamations. Set new goals for yourself when you need to, and repeat the entire process each time you need to update your budget.

WORKING WITH SPIRITS
in Prosperity Magic

> ***Spirits:*** Abundantia, Aine, Brigantia, Daikoku, Danu, Demeter, Eopa, Fortuna, Freya, Ganesh, Hathor, Jambala, Juno, Jupiter, Lakshmi, Mercury, Oshun, Teutates, Veles, Venus

Just because money isn't a natural phenomenon doesn't mean that it doesn't have a spiritual presence. Anything we humans invest psychic energy into becomes some sort of spiritual entity, and money has accumulated a lot of psychic energy over the years. I personally work with a few spiritual entities that rule over finances, most notably the goddess Fortuna, daughter of Jupiter. I put up an altar for her and started making regular offerings, and before I knew it, she was opening up doors left and right.

Regardless of the spirits you are personally working with at the moment, they should all be on board for your financial growth and success. Use the spirit sigil below to bring focus to the energies of your spirits and direct them toward the manifestation of your desired goals.

Fortuna is a very opulent force who prefers to be given the very finest you have to offer. My partners and I adore her so much that we have created an altar for her right next to the hearth. We have noticed she has an affinity for yellow flowers, sunflowers, and champagne. She likes to get flowers that are almost in bloom so that they open and reveal their beauty on her altar. She prefers to have a statue that has been consecrated in her name; however, you can begin your relationship by drawing the black sigil on the next page in gold on a black piece of paper and placing it on your altar as a quintessential anchor. As soon as you can, though, get her a statue.

Every day upon visiting your money altar, recite the following enchantment to draw her energy into your life. Once you begin this work, every one of your major financial successes and achievements, no matter how large or small, should be devoted to her. Simply toast to her and say, "Hail, Fortuna!" I also put my wallet right-side up on her altar every night when I get home. I place it in such a way that the fold where the money goes is facing upward and ask her to pour cash into it, especially when it is empty.

The Prayer of Fortuna

Fortuna, you who are truly full of grace,
You who are blessed among all those with want for a better life,
You whose feet drip gold and whose hands carry plenty,
I call upon your power: come now and bring the floods of your blessing.

Regardless of the spirits you work with, use the Fortuna symbol on the following page to bring all of their energy into focus. Draw it in green or red ink and put it in your loose change jar, piggy bank, or check register to attract larger sums of money. Etch it onto green candles to bring clarity regarding financial decisions and manifest financial goals.

Fortuna loves yellow flowers, sunflowers, and champagne.

Hail, Fortuna!

WORKING WITH SYMBOLS AND SYNCHRONICITY
in Prosperity Magic

> ***Tarot Cards:*** Wheel of Fortune, The Sun, Ace of Pentacles, Ten of Pentacles, Queen of Pentacles, King of Pentacles

Prosperity comes in many faces, and this may be seen in detail throughout the tarot. While several of the cards could help you to steer the trajectory of your financial goals, there are a few that I keep coming back to over and over again for this magic.

The entire suit of pentacles speaks of prosperity and wealth, but the Ace, Ten, King, and Queen of Pentacles are excellent to work with for magic that takes place over time or according to business cycles. Burn corresponding incense and place the cards on your altar under the full or new moon to help trigger their cycles. The Ace of Pentacles can be used to summon new opportunities in a field or a new job at a new location. The Ten of Pentacles invokes stability and abundant opportunity. The Queen of Pentacles can be worked with to call for assistance from Human Resources or to get a raise. The King of Pentacles, on the other hand, helps to forge new partnerships and investments.

The Sun is an excellent card to take with you on job interviews. Put the Wheel of Fortune under a candle holder and then light a green candle on top of it to help when seeking assistance with debt.

> ***Numbers:*** 3, 5, 7, 11, 13, 21, 44, 55, 77, 99, 100

Numbers appear in prosperity magic usually to symbolize blessings, the fruits of labor, or straight-up good luck. Any of the numbers listed here can be used in prosperity magic to help increase the flow of abundant streams of income. Chant the name of Fortuna one hundred times to gain her favor. Light seven birthday candles to make a wish (even when it's not your birthday). Look for the numbers 11, 13, 21, and 44 to appear as omens of good fortune.

CROWN OF SUCCESS WITCH'S CORD

A powerful way to work with numbers in prosperity magic is by making a witch's cord. This type of spell is believed to be one of the oldest forms of magic in the Western world and is performed to bring various elements into harmony so that a particular desire can be fulfilled. A witch's cord is essentially an altar made from rope that has various spells and amulets tied to it. The knotting binds the spells together to form what could be thought of as a sort of ultra-spell with multiple cogs working in tandem.

To make one, we follow much the same principle as the love knot spell we did in chapter 3 but on a much bigger scale. In that spell, each charm and knot represented a point of focus that led to the spell's completion. With this working, we will need to create smaller spells—like charm bags, spell bottles, or amulets—and work with their combined strength over a period of time. Think of each component like a part of the team, with each member bringing their power to the game. To make a cord like the one pictured here, tie thirteen prosperity spells together to a green cord of three yards. You can work with as many component spells as you feel called to, and you can even add tarot cards, gemstones, and other correspondences as part of the working. This is a slower type of working and is one of my favorites. It may take time to make each part, but the results will be worth it. I recommend beginning with three, five, or seven spells, and then adding to the cord over time. Think of them like cloth altars!

When finished, hang it in the sun for three days. At dusk on the final day, say: "By the powers of the mighty sun, success shall be mine! By the powers of the mighty sun, success shall be here! By the powers of the mighty sun, success has already come! So must it be!" Hang the cord somewhere prominent.

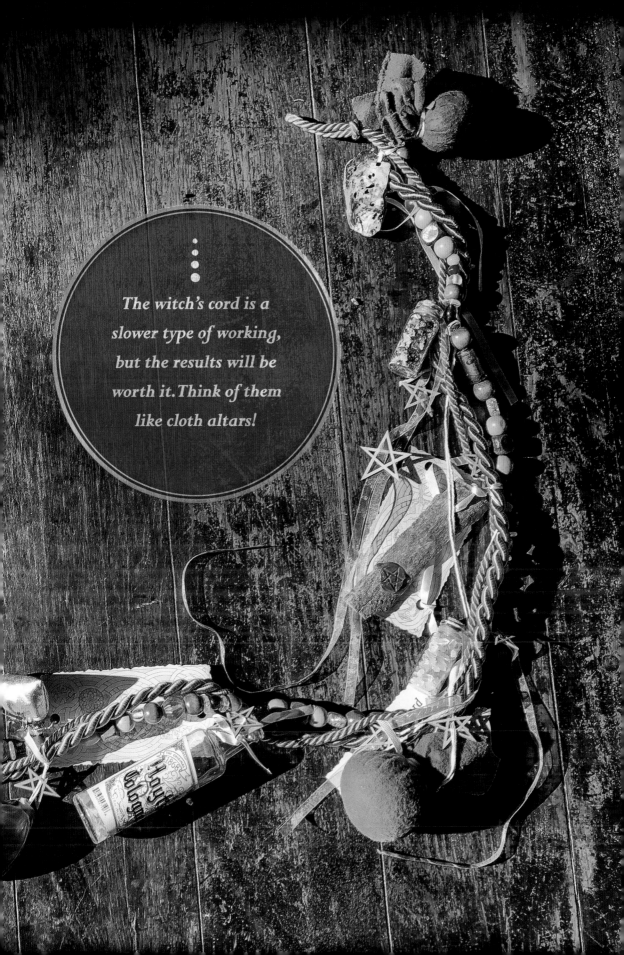

The witch's cord is a slower type of working, but the results will be worth it. Think of them like cloth altars!

> *Animals and Insects:* ant, bat, bee, boar, bull, buffalo, carp/koi, cat, cattle of any kind, deer, dog (especially black), eagle, elephant, frog, goldfish, horse, lion, peacock, pig, stag, tiger, toad

When working with the animal kingdom, we would likely work with species who have a regal, majestic nature or are known for their industry, such as ants and bees. Speaking of bees, in chapter 3 we discussed the use of a honey jar spell (see pages 113–118).

> *A honey jar can also be used for prosperity workings, the idea being that (A) money will sweeten up to you and (B) people will be attracted to you and want to give you money.*

When working a honey jar for prosperity, however, you will want to include a piece of honeycomb. You can find jars of honey with the comb in most health food stores or online. Working with the comb will add extra bee energy to your magic.

During part two, instead of writing a person's name, write the word "prosperous"; continue to write your name as instructed. The circle around the script should read something like "Money, come to me; money, set me free; money, stay with me!" Instead of hearts in the corners, draw dollar signs. Dress with prosperity condition oil.

During part three, follow all instructions; once you have the honey on your tongue, say, "By sweet honey and sugar bee, money and prosperity will come to me!"

During part four, use green or gold candles instead, though red will work as well. Dress with prosperity condition oil and incense.

Prosperity looks different for every culture, but usually it is associated with the color of money, no matter where you are. In general, gold and green tend to be used most in American folk magic.

One of my favorite spells for harnessing the flow of foot traffic in and out of your home or business for money is to tie an enchanted green ribbon onto the door. Take a yard of green ribbon and dress the tips with prosperity condition oil. Every time someone moves through the door, the ribbon will sway in the air and pick up a charge. Under every full moon, dunk the ribbon into a bowl of water and allow the moonlight to empower it overnight. In the morning, remove the ribbon and hang to dry, then add the remaining water to a prosperity bath.

Iconography: coins (especially foreign), cornucopia, crown of success, dollar sign, Fehu rune, gold brick, horseshoe, pentacle, seventh pentacle of Jupiter, pentagram, phallus, pyramid, rainbow

This grouping of symbols can be used in your prosperity magic to help manifest your goals of financial freedom and security. Working with any one of these symbols will lend special energy to your workings.

Place a cornucopia on your altar to symbolize your gratitude to the spirits you work with for all of the abundance and prosperity they have brought into your life. Draw a gold pentagram in workings meant to bring out the value in something. Hang a horseshoe on your door to draw financial luck to your home. Place a crystal phallus under a water fountain to encourage new business.

Make a money charm bag and carry it with you to attract prosperity. To a green, red, or gold swatch of fabric, add three pinches comfrey, three pennies, and a small piece of paper that has the seventh pentacle of Jupiter drawn on it in gold ink. Before placing the paper in the bag, dress it with three drops prosperity condition oil. Tie together tightly with white or gold thread.

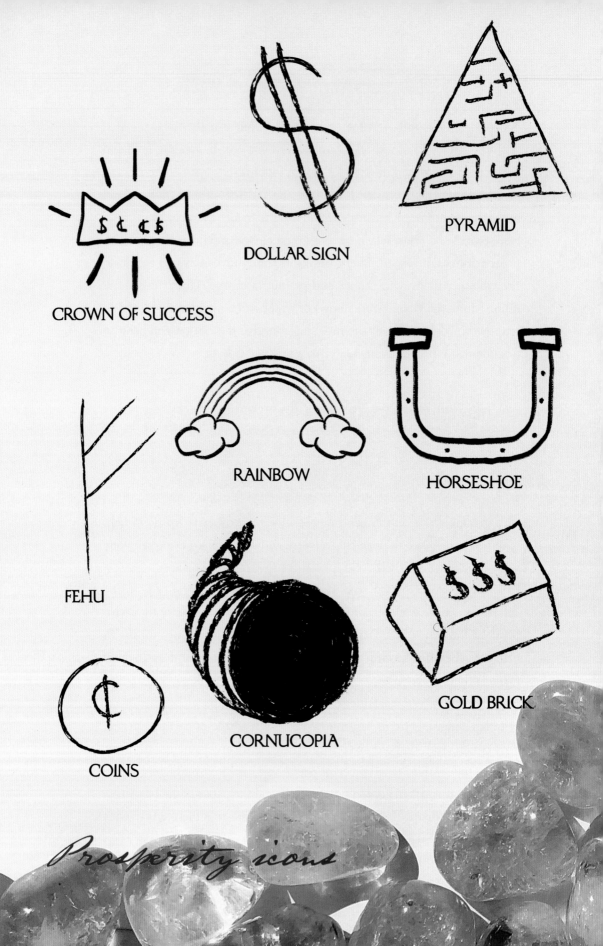

CROWN OF SUCCESS

DOLLAR SIGN

PYRAMID

FEHU

RAINBOW

HORSESHOE

COINS

CORNUCOPIA

GOLD BRICK

Prosperity icons

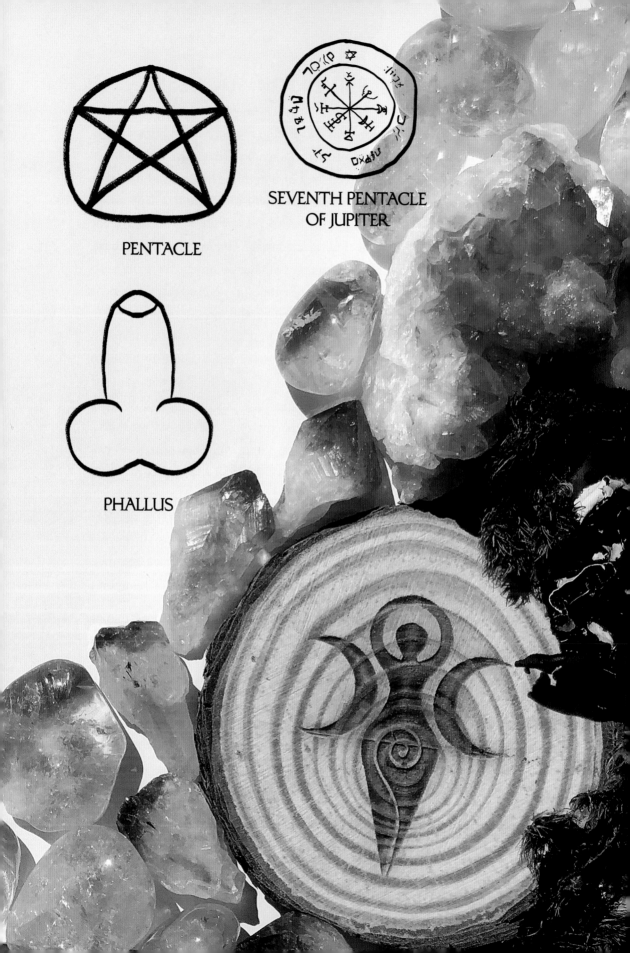

PENTACLE

SEVENTH PENTACLE
OF JUPITER

PHALLUS

HIMMELSBRIEF FOR SUCCESS

The Himmelsbrief, or "heaven's letter," is an old spell from Germany that falls under the category of declaration magic. Said to miraculously fall from heaven, the Himmelsbrief is a magical certificate that declares the bearer to be protected from evil or blessed by heaven, and it usually contains some sort of contractual agreement to ensure this happens. In return for the favors of heaven, the bearer must abide by a set of agreed-upon ethics, all of which is clearly stated in the Himmelsbrief. For example, one might agree to pay 10 percent of their income to a charity, feed the poor, help the homeless, or invest time in a cause that will benefit their community in exchange for supernatural favor.

This is a very powerful act of magic that should not be undertaken lightly. By creating and signing the Himmelsbrief, you are agreeing to a bargain. All witches are warned about entering into bargains with the spiritual world; do so respectfully and with every intention of fulfilling your end. If you agree to donate to charity, you must do so. If you agree to volunteer time, you must do so. To not follow through once the blessings start to roll in would instantly break the spell and usually results in the loss of whatever it is that you gained, if not more. The only risk you take is by not following through.

This spell has many different variations and came my way by witches who practice Pow-wow, or Pennsylvanian Dutch Folk Magic. In their version, the Himmelsbrief is often kept on their person or hung on a wall to imbue the space with its properties, and it contains passages from the Bible, as the Bible is seen as a talisman all of its own. Our Himmelsbrief will not require the use of Bible verses, but traditionally Psalm 72 and Psalm 144 make excellent additions. Not all witches like to use the Bible in their workings, and this is one instance where we can respectfully get away with not using it if you have an aversion. Write the psalms on the back of the Himmelsbrief if you would like to add their magic.

What You Will Need

- black tea (to create tea stain)
- 1 cup water
- yellow marker (not pictured)
- the sigil of Fortuna:

- 7 x 7-inch piece of parchment paper
- black, green, or gold ink pen
- paintbrush
- gold acrylic paint
- prosperity incense

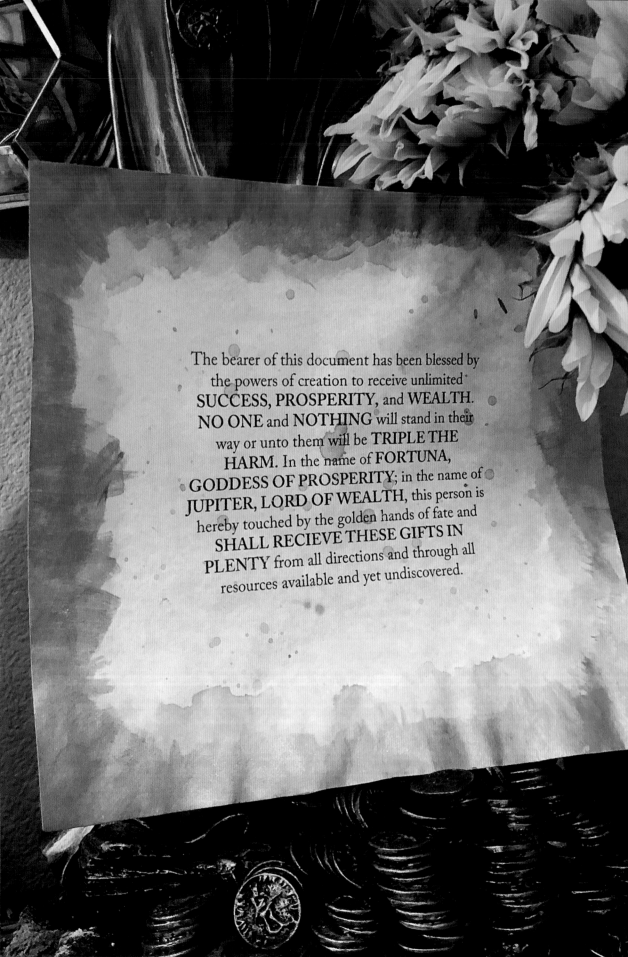

The bearer of this document has been blessed by the powers of creation to receive unlimited SUCCESS, PROSPERITY, and WEALTH. NO ONE and NOTHING will stand in their way or unto them will be TRIPLE THE HARM. In the name of FORTUNA, GODDESS OF PROSPERITY; in the name of JUPITER, LORD OF WEALTH, this person is hereby touched by the golden hands of fate and SHALL RECIEVE THESE GIFTS IN PLENTY from all directions and through all resources available and yet undiscovered.

Create the Himmelsbrief

Make a tea stain by brewing a double-strength cup of black tea. Allow it to steep until it becomes room temperature. While the tea steeps, draw the sigil of Fortuna in the center of the parchment paper with a yellow marker.

Write the following prayer incantation over the sigil in black ink:

> *The bearer of this document has been blessed by*
> *the powers of creation to receive unlimited*
> **SUCCESS, PROSPERITY,** *and* **WEALTH***.*
> **NO ONE** *and* **NOTHING** *will stand in their*
> *way or unto them will be* **TRIPLE THE**
> **HARM***. In the name of* **FORTUNA,**
> **GODDESS OF PROSPERITY***, and in the name of*
> **JUPITER, LORD OF WEALTH***, this person is*
> *hereby touched by the golden hands of fate and*
> **SHALL RECIEVE THESE GIFTS IN**
> **PLENTY** *from all directions and through all*
> *resources available and yet undiscovered.*

Using your paintbrush, stain the outer one to two inches of the paper. Set aside to dry.

Once dried, paint the outer half-inch edge of the paper gold. Set aside to dry.

Ignite the prosperity incense and wave the Himmelsbrief through the smoke seven times while you repeat the incantation each time. After the final pass, say, "So must this be!"

Hang the Himmelsbrief or carry it with you and replace as necessary.

Chapter 7
DIVINATION

The arts of divination aren't so much acts of bewitchment as they are methods of gathering information that we use in our magic. While it certainly helps to have psychic abilities, there is little that tends to be psychic about the practice of divination. We do, however, work with divination as psychic people to help amplify and clarify our psychic connection to the world around us. That being said, anyone can learn how to divine.

Witches use divination for all sorts of reasons. It allows us to check in on people and situations with as much detail as we might need. It gives us the ability to foretell the future by sequencing the likely chain of events to follow, it can tell us of someone's true intentions, and it can help us contact those on the other side. Some methods are direct and leave room for creative interpretations, whereas others come with strict rules and require traditional training.

Divination is interesting in that the methods we employ for it have continued to evolve with every generation that gets its hands on them. As we will explore in this chapter, many of the methods overlap and share symbolism; this is because we have a long history of sticking to what works. More important than any herb, gemstone, or oil we could make, the language of symbolism is perhaps the most important aspect of divination there is.

DISCERNMENT

Along with divination comes discernment, which is the ability to judge whether or not the information is useful and how that information can be applied to the situation. It is a valuable skill that requires time to develop. The more you practice and explore methods, the better you will become at discernment. Fortunately, most systems of divination come with information that helps with this. For discernment to be useful, we must rely on our instinct and intuition. There is no harm in looking things up to get guidance, but in the end you must ask yourself how that information applies and then listen to that voice in the back of your head.

There are hundreds of official methods of divination and countless methods that have never been recorded. Of these methods, there are a handful to know and perform that are considered standard among witches. In this chapter we will take a look at these methods as well as how correspondences can be used with them.

WORKING WITH THE MINERAL KINGDOM
in Divination

Minerals and Gemstones: amber, amethyst, angelite, aquamarine, azurite, celestite, dumortierite, fluorite, iolite, jet, kyanite, labradorite, lapis lazuli, larimar, moldavite, moonstone (especially black and rainbow varieties), opal, quartz (especially clear and rutilated varieties), selenite, seraphinite, sodalite, sugilite, tanzanite, tiger's eye, wulfenite

Metals: brass, copper, silver

Aside from scrying, we will primarily work with the mineral kingdom for its ability to assist the mental and psychic processes. Each one of the stones listed here is capable of helping you gather and make sense of information via divinatory means. This is especially true of azurite, dumortierite, larimar, opal, and wulfenite.

Angelite, celestite, labradorite, selenite, seraphinite, and wulfenite will connect you to high-vibrational spirits such as guides, ascended masters, and angels. Amber, jet, lapis lazuli, rutilated quartz, and sodalite will assist in opening channels of communication with ancestors and the spirits of the departed. Wear amber and jet to increase psychic acuity during divination as well as to protect you from unwanted spirits.

Keep a piece of amethyst, aquamarine, dumortierite, kyanite, moonstone, or selenite with you to help gently open the psychic and mental centers—excellent to use in meditation prior to workings as well as during them. Black moonstone can be worked with to help you see aspects of yourself and others that normally remain hidden; work with it to reveal the truth.

Clear quartz can be used to help amplify your psychic and mental abilities. Wear a piece around your neck to bring clarity to the shamanic and spiritual, especially when performing magic. Sleep with a piece of clear quartz next to your head to help bring definition to your dreams. Amethyst will help ward off nightmares.

Work with kyanite, labradorite, quartz, sodalite, sugilite, and tanzanite to aid in the processes of discernment. Kyanite and labradorite can be placed on the altar to encourage general enhancement of discernment in addition to helping establish an energetic connection between you and another person.

SCRYING

Scrying is perhaps the easiest and likely the oldest form of divination. It involves gazing into or at an object and discerning symbols. It is actually a bit more complicated than that, as you might imagine. The technique is to gaze and then slip into a light trance where symbols, shapes, and scenes will appear either in your line of sight or in your mind. It is a lot like getting lost in thought and staring off into space. The trick, however, is to be observant of what you perceive while doing so and to allow the information to flow to you without force. You can scry into anything, but it does take some practice to get the hang of it.

The mineral kingdom assists us with mental and psychic processes, and heightens our intuitive abilities.

The most popular method of scrying involves gazing into a reflective surface, such as a mirror, pool of water, or crystal/gemstone. Mirrors and water are effective and easy to find, but there is something special about working with the mineral kingdom when scrying.

Crystal balls generally are made from crystal glass, which has a high lead content and is not actually a gemstone like quartz. There have been methods developed, however, to "reconstitute" some stones. Reconstitution involves melting down the stone and then reforming it into a desired shape. In the end, it doesn't really matter too much which type of crystal ball you pick, as long as it works for you. I do find that working with a natural crystal sphere works best for me. Because scrying relies more on your ability to drift off into a meditative/trance state, I prefer to work with gemstones that assist in the psychic processes, like those listed above.

Truthfully, you can scry into anything from wallpaper to the clouds, and you probably have already done this a million times without thinking about it. What I present to you here is a quick formal rundown of the process, but I encourage you not to overthink it or make it harder on yourself than necessary. In the beginning I thought I was messing it up, but I realized it was an incredibly gentle process, not one that can be forced. In my example, we will be working with a crystal ball; however, know that for this type of exercise, you really only need what we refer to as a "point of fascination," or something solid to look at, preferably with a reflective surface.

One of the difficulties with scrying lies in the need to trust yourself and what you see. The moment you question it, you have already lost connection to it. It is important to just let it come and to observe it as it does; you can discern what it all means when it is over.

Scrying in Five Easy Steps

1 Place a crystal ball on a stable, flat surface and dim the lights as much as possible. You might prefer to turn the lights all the way off and then light two or three candles to provide ambient light.

2 Sit comfortably in front of the sphere and take nine deep and steady breaths. While you do this, allow distractions to melt away and bring yourself entirely into the moment.

3 Look into the very center of the ball and continue to breathe slowly and deeply. While you do this, let your peripheral vision shift out of focus until the only thing that you can clearly see is the point of fascination at the center of the sphere.

4 At this point you very well might start to receive images and impressions. If not, then there are two things to do:

- Visualize a television or theater screen at the center of the stone. Sometimes this helps with seeing the other images.

- While you gaze, visualize the center of the stone in your mind and allow images to appear that way.

5 Allow any information to come in the form of images, physical sensations, or sounds. When you feel yourself losing focus or the connection fading, simply end the session by closing your eyes and taking three deep breaths. When you open them again, immediately look at something else.

PENDULUMS

A form of dowsing, working with pendulums is a long-held tradition among mystics and witches that may go back over five thousand years. A pendulum can be made by attaching any type of weight to a cord or thin chain. The pendulum's chain is then held and the weight is allowed to sway on its own, without direct physical instruction from the user. Its motions are then interpreted. The belief is that human sensitivity is enhanced by use of the pendulum, allowing us to identify any source of radiant energy that we might be looking for. In truth, it is more likely that the pendulum works best as an extension of your subconscious, as the movements are actually caused by the flexing of tiny muscles in your hand. This doesn't mean the pendulum isn't valuable; on the contrary, it means that it can have a very personal connection to the user.

Yes and No with a Pendulum

Any one of the minerals listed here would make an excellent pendulum, especially clear quartz and copper. Once you have selected your pendulum, hold it so that the weight is about a foot away from your solar plexus and command the pendulum to stop moving. Before we can ask it questions, we need to establish the language of its movements. When the pendulum stops moving, command it to show you what yes looks like. The pendulum should begin to sway back and forth or possibly even move in a circular motion. Once it does, command it to stop, and then command it to show you what no looks like. Once it does, command it to stop. If you get the same motion for both yes and no, then you need to start over. If you got two different responses, then begin asking the pendulum a set of test questions that you already know the answer to, such as "Is my favorite color blue?" or "Does the sun rise in the east?" After yes and no have been established, you can go forward with other yes-or-no questions of your choosing.

Pendulums are extentions
of your subconscious

WORKING WITH THE PLANT KINGDOM
in Divination

> ***Plants, Herbs, and Trees:*** alder, anise, apple, ash, bay, beech, birch, blackberry, blackthorn, bracken, calendula, camphor, cedar, cinquefoil, coffee, coltsfoot, white copal, cypress, dandelion, eyebright, galangal, grains of paradise, gravel root, hazel, holly, honeysuckle, huckleberry, hyssop, jasmine, juniper, lemon balm, magnolia, marigold, mastic, mugwort, mullein, myrrh, myrtle, oak, onion, peppermint, pine, pomegranate, rowan, saffron, tea (any), thyme, tobacco, uva ursa, walnut, wormwood, yarrow, yerba santa

Keep bay on your person to assist in clear pathways of communication when you perform a reading or consult a psychic. Similarly, put bay in your shoe to keep yourself from being psychically detected.

Jasmine, lemon balm, marigold, and thyme should be grown near the front door to encourage fresh energy in the home. Add peppermint or onion to ward off negative spirits. A charm bag can be made with all six of these ingredients to keep you safe from spirit attachments when working with other people.

Collect fresh juniper berries and leave them near the hearth to encourage communication from your ancestors.

MULLEIN AND MUGWORT
FINGER SCRYING SPELL

At night when the moon is waning or new, take a solid-colored plate and to it add enough dried mullein and mugwort to cover the center of the plate. Align and center your energy, and then place the index finger of your dominant hand in the center of the plate. Close your eyes and say,

Mullein and mugwort, be true to me
Show me what I cannot see.

Take a deep breath and then allow your index finger to move freely of its own accord for a few moments. As your finger moves, it will carve a path through the herbs. Open your eyes and look at the design your finger made. Scry into the symbol as instructed earlier in the chapter and record it for later work.

TASSEOMANCY

The art of tea leaf or coffee ground reading goes back to possibly the thirteenth century and is a staple for diehard diviners. It is an incredibly simple method that is known for providing direct and no-nonsense information. It does, however, leave plenty of room for interpretation and discernment. The trick to this is not to use teabags, as you want there to be herb particles in the water.

When brewing coffee and reading the grounds, the use of a French press is ideal. Pour the tea/coffee into a cup and enjoy! It helps to add a bit of sugar, which will help the particles at the bottom stick to the cup at the end. When you are finished drinking, try to let the particles dry a bit, if possible, then look into the cup and see if any symbols pop out to you. A list of symbols is provided later in this chapter.

By my witch eye
I see the hidden world

Herbs and spices known to clear the mind are all commonly used in divination magic. The same can be said for those that help relax the body.

DIVINATION INCENSE

Combine and powder ⅓ ounce each white copal, jasmine, and cedar tips. Make on Monday or Wednesday. Burn over charcoal to imbue your workings with enhanced psychic abilities or as a working all its own to encourage general psychic clarity.

Variations

To Communicate with the Dead: Substitute copal with myrrh. Add ⅓ ounce frankincense and ⅓ ounce mullein. Burn before and after work with the dead and on All Hallows.

To Clarify and Strengthen Visions: Add ⅓ ounce dragon's blood and ¼ ounce oak. Make only on Wednesday, preferably under the waxing or full moon. Burn at dusk for best results.

For Prophecy and Oracular Work: Substitute cedar with cypress. Add ⅓ ounce eyebright and ⅓ ounce lavender. Blend under a full moon. Burn when needed or regularly on Wednesday nights to encourage prophetic dreaming.

Soothsaying and Communicating with the Gods: Substitute copal with frankincense. Add ⅓ ounce mugwort, ⅓ ounce myrrh, and ¼ ounce yarrow. Blend during the daytime when the moon is full. Burn during or before related work.

To Aid in Prediction and Forecast: Substitute cedar tips with hyssop. Add ⅓ ounce dragon's blood. Burn when needed.

> **Essential Oils:** bay, calendula, carnation, cedar, clary sage, cypress, frankincense, galangal, heliotrope, hyssop, jasmine, lavender, lemongrass, mugwort, myrrh, orris, rose, rosemary, rue, sandalwood, thyme

PSYCHIC CONDITION OIL

In a ½ ounce bottle, combine the following essential oils to make a psychic condition oil: 13 drops myrrh, 9 drops cedar, and 7 drops hyssop. Add a small pinch of eyebright or honeysuckle to the bottle. Fill the rest of the bottle with carrier oil and mix well.

Sometimes there are specific conditions that require a small modification to the original recipe so that we cane hone in on the right issues. Here are five other psychic oils that you can make to help you do just that. Make these adjustments before adding carrier oil.

> ***To Heighten ESP:*** Add 3 drops carnation essential oil. Dab on wrists after a spiritual alignment and prior to psychic work.
>
> ***To Clarify Internal Energy Channels and Enhance Premonitions:*** Add 5 drops lemongrass essential oil. Apply to wrists and behind ears before scrying.
>
> ***To Communicate with the Deceased:*** Replace hyssop essential oil with clary sage essential oil and add a pinch of willow bark to the bottle instead of the eyebright or honeysuckle. Under the new moon, write the name of the departed you wish to make contact with three times on a 5 x 5-inch square of parchment paper. Write the names so that they are in a column, one under the other like a stack. Using a paintbrush or your index finger, dress the paper by painting an X over the block of names with the oil. Put this under a black candle and burn at midnight to attract that specific spirit to you.
>
> ***For Prophetic Dreams:*** Substitute cedar essential oil with cypress essential oil. Add 5 drops lavender essential oil. Apply one to two drops onto the bottom of your feet before bed.
>
> ***For Personal Psychic Aftercare:*** Add 9 drops lemongrass essential oil and 5 drops honeysuckle essential oil. Blend under the full moon.

Divination requires us to let
go of everything that might be
keeping us from being in the moment.
To help them relinquish outside concerns
and bring focus to the now, many witches
work with the aromatherapeutic
properties of essential oils such
as catnip, jasmine, lavender,
and oud.

WORKING WITH COSMIC FORCES
in Divination

> ***Houses and Signs:*** all, especially
> Aquarius, Capricorn, Pisces, Sagittarius
> ***Planets:*** all, especially Mercury, Moon, Pluto, Uranus
> ***Days:*** Sunday, Monday, Wednesday, Friday

Each house and planet is connected to various aspects of divination. Those listed here are especially known for having a heavy psychic influence. For those who struggle with divination, work with Mercury, Pluto, and Uranus to bring much-needed depth and clarity to your sessions.

LUNAR MEDITATION TO INCREASE INTUITION

The moon rules over intuition and can be allied with to increase sensitivity during divination. To do this, perform the following lunar meditation on Monday evenings to get a weekly dose of the moon's powerful energy.

Find a dark place, sit comfortably, and close your eyes. Visualize yourself sitting in the room, totally surrounded by the darkness. See the full moon over your head, lighting the darkness and drawing your attention to it. Take a deep breath and visualize the light from the moon intensifying and then pouring into you. Allow the light to fill you completely, and as it does so, see that you begin to radiate with the light of the moon. Once you are filled up, see the moonlight stop pouring into you and the moon rising off into the sky. For a few moments, allow yourself to hold the light that was poured into you and simply feel that power. As you radiate with the light of the moon, so too does your intuition. After a few moments, open your eyes; the meditation is done.

WORKING WITH SPIRITS
in Divination

Spirits: Anulap, Apollo, Aradia, Aset, Astarte, Auriel, Diana, Egeria, the Fata/Fates, Freya, Gabriel, Gamayun, Ganesh, Hecate, Heka, Hermes, Innana, Janus, Jupiter/Zeus, Lucifer, Mercury, Metatron, Neptune, Norns, Odin, Thoth

Working with spirits is often implied in divination, but those listed here are associated with psychic power as well as divination. Each of them is known for bestowing their followers with the gifts of foresight and prophecy. Use this symbol in your magic to gather the focus of all the spirits you work with to aid you in your divination practices. Simply draw it on paper and stare into it for a few minutes while you picture yourself opening up to receiving messages from the spirit world. Alternatively, etch it into the side of a candle and gaze into the flame before divination to connect with its intention.

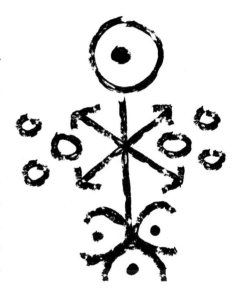

SPIRIT BOARDS

Spirit boards, also known as witch or Ouija boards, have an interesting history that started out in the Spiritualist movement at the turn of the twentieth century. Originally, they were designed by the faithful to help initiate contact with their deceased loved ones and relatives. They were worked with for decades without incident until the movie *The Exorcist* came out. Anyone familiar with the movie knows that the plot revolves around a demonic possession that begins by using a spirit board. After the movie came out, the use of spirit boards skyrocketed—and so did myths of nefarious happenings.

Fire, walk with me

Spirit boards are tools that help by creating a direct line of communication wherein the spirit can spell out their responses. Like any magical tool, they require intention to work. If you approach a board with the intention of meeting your ancestor, then that will be what happens. But if you approach the board just for fun and have no specific spirit in mind, you are likely to get any number of random spirits picking up the line instead. Having a specific person or entity in mind before approaching the board will increase your chances of having a safe, effective session.

Five Easy Steps to Working the Spirit Board

1 Set the board down on a level, flat surface, and place the planchette in the center of the board. Take a few deep breaths. Think about the person you want to talk to and visualize them in your mind.

2 Say the person's name aloud five times and visualize them walking toward you and meeting you at the spirit board.

3 Put two or three fingers from your dominant hand onto the planchette. Close your eyes.

4 Gently push or pull the planchette in any direction that feels natural to you for as long as feels natural to you. When it feels instinctive to do so, stop moving the planchette and open your eyes to see where you stopped. Record the number or letter, then close your eyes and repeat until satisfied.

5 When it is time to end the session, move the planchette to the word "goodbye" or to the center of the board and remove your hand. Visualize the spirit with whom you communicated, thank them for their time, and then tell them it is time to end the session. Visualize them walking away from you in the direction they came from. Open your eyes and then knock on the board three times to end the connection.

WORKING WITH SYMBOLS
AND SYNCHRONICITY
in Divination

More important than anything else in divination is the language of symbolism. The study of symbols and synchronicities makes up the bulk of the divinatory arts. In this section we will look at ways to work with symbolism and synchronicity to enhance your divination as well as ways to interpret them.

> ***Tarot Cards:*** all, especially the High Priestess, Wheel of Fortune, and Judgement

A form of cartomancy, tarot is perhaps one of the most popular types of divination; there are thousands of books on the subject, not to mention YouTube videos and blogs. There is no lack of knowledge when it comes to the tarot, as it is all freely available for anyone who has a deck to work with. While we won't be covering the meanings of the tarot cards in this book, in the bibliography there is a list of books that I highly recommend on the subject.

The cards listed here, however, can be used to help increase your divinatory talents. The High Priestess will help you understand the meanings of symbols and connect the dots between them. Judgement will help you to discover and empower any unknown psychic or intuitive skill. The Wheel of Fortune can aid in opening up the psychic centers.

> *Place these cards—the High Priestess, Wheel of Fortune, and Judgement—on your altar or in your Book of Shadows to draw focus and attention to your intuitive abilities.*

Iconography: all-seeing eye, asterisk, feather, goddess, key, Mercury, moon, open hand, pentacle, triple moon, wheel

Divination is, in so many ways, all about the symbolism, and this chapter is a big example of that. The iconography I list here represent symbolism that can be employed in your workings to enhance your psychic and divinatory skills. Apply the glyph of Mercury to clarify your ability to receive messages from the spirit world as well as to understand the meaning of omens. Etch the glyph of the moon onto candles to see through illusion. Draw the all-seeing eye on parchment and then sprinkle it with divination incense before rolling the paper into a tube and tossing it into a fire to bring about images in the flame.

TRIPLE MOON

FEATHER

OPEN HAND

ALL-SEEING EYE

Divination icons

ASTERISK

KEY

MERCURY

MOON

PENTACLE

GODDESS

WHEEL

> ***Numbers:*** 1, 3, 9, 11, 13, 44, 56, 78, 101

Numbers often come up in divination, and they each have their own meanings. When you see the numbers listed here out in the wild, however, they indicate the need to perform an act of divination—as though someone or something were trying to get your attention. The numbers 1, 11, 44, and 78 are related to angelic forces and spirit teachers. Numbers 3, 9, and 13 are associated with the dead. Numbers 56, 78, and 101 are associated with major life change.

> ***Animals and Insects:*** boar, blue jay, butterfly, crow, goose, dog, fox, horse, hummingbird, lynx, mantis, magpie, mole, moth, owl, peacock, rabbit, raven, snake, toad, wolf, wren

Animals and insects, especially those listed here, often appear in divination. To see an animal that lives in the water is a sign of emotional need and healing. To see one that flies is to be warned of news to come. To see a reptile is to be told of health troubles on the way or be warned of being double-crossed. To see a mammal is to be warned of family concerns.

> ***Colors:*** black, blue, gold, indigo, lavender, purple, silver, violet, white, yellow

Color has a prominent place in divination because it is chock-full of symbolism. Reference the chart in chapter 2 for a quick list of colors and their meanings so you know what to specifically look out for. Otherwise, the colors listed here can be incorporated into your workings to help you with your divination. Silver is an excellent color for piercing through illusion and seeing the truth. Perform your readings on a purple cloth to heighten your ability to focus and discern. Light blue grabs the attention of high-vibrational spirits like angels and some faeries. Wear black and wrap your divination tools in black to keep safe from negative energy. Wear white to bring clarity to your visions.

CARTOMANCY

Cartomancy—the use of cards for divination—is by far the most popular system of all. We've all been exposed to the tarot, but most people don't know that it got its start as a simple deck of playing cards. The major arcana was added later, but you can still use just a regular deck of playing cards for divination. The Lenormand is a system that developed in Germany and then later became popularized when it was named after a famous French psychic, Madame Lenormand, after her death in the mid-nineteenth century. The cards took common symbols used in divination and combined them with specific playing cards. Interestingly enough, the symbols used in the Lenormand are the same symbols used in tea leaf/coffee ground reading, also known as tasseomancy.

Use the following "diviner's chart" to discern the meaning of these three systems.

PC	Number	Lenormand	Meaning
A♦	31	Sun	Success, wealth, positive outcome
2♦			Exchange of wealth or property
3♦			Unexpected gifts
4♦			Accounts, wallet, purse
5♦			Luck and chance
6♦	2	Clover	Good luck, blessings, positive choices
7♦	12	Bird(s)	Gossip, misunderstandings, lies
8♦	33	Key	Opportunity, changing of circumstances
9♦	8	Coffin	An absolute ending, completion
10♦	26	Book	Information, knowledge, secrets

PC	Number	Lenormand	Meaning
J♦	10	Scythe	Harvest, clearing a path, seperation
Q♦	22	Path/ Crossroad	Important Decisions, Fork in road
K♦	34	Fish	Prosperous work and finances
A♣	25	Ring	Connection, Partnership, Marriage
2♣			New allies or friendships
3♣			Obstacles with current friends, arguments
4♣			Hard work and physical labor
5♣			Physical body and health
6♣	36	Cross	Burden, weight, stress
7♣	23	Mice	Missing information, lies
8♣	21	Mountain	Obstacles and challenges
9♣	14	Fox	Need to move forward carefully, move with cunning
10♣	15	Bear	Career, job, authority, power
J♣	11	Whip	Punishment, discipline, unrest
Q♣	7	Snake	Someone close is up to no good
K♣	6	Cloud	Confusion, frustration
A♥	28	Man	Someone who identifies as male
2♥			New romance, sex
3♥			Happiness, wishes granted
4♥			Loyalty and trust
5♥			Fertility and pregnancy
6♥	16	Star	Hope, looking ahead, planning
7♥	5	Tree	Traditions, lineage, values

PC	Number	Lenormand	Meaning
8♥	32	Moon	High emotions, suspicion
9♥	1	Rider	New beginning, inspiration
10♥	18	Dog	True friendship, plutonic love
J♥	24	Heart	True love, hot romance, spiritual connection
Q♥	17	Stork	Big news, pregnancy, new things coming
K♥	4	House/ Doorway	Security, safety, sanctuary
A♠	29	Woman	Someone who identifies as female
2♠			Separation, arguments, polarization
3♠			Fighting, setbacks, battle
4♠			Fear mongering, enemies, do not trust
5♠			Illness, disease, possible death
6♠	19	Tower	Need for awareness, distraction, temptations
7♠	27	Letter	Important news, email, message
8♠	20	Garden	Social engagements, community, party
9♠	35	Anchor	Hope, stability, capability, safety
10♠	3	Ship	Movement, journey, adventure
J♠	13	Child	An actual child
Q♠	9	Flowers	New happiness or reason to celebrate, joy
K♠	30	Lily	Sex, purity, queer people

Spirits above, below, within—
Be here now and let
the work begin

Beginner's Cartomancy

It is easy to make cartomancy complicated, but by design it is a straight-forward and user-friendly way to perform divination. All you need is a deck of either tarot, oracle, playing, or Lenormand cards and time to learn. The most difficult aspect of this form of divination is tying the pieces together. Let's take a look at a handful of useful spreads that will help you develop that skill.

A few things to keep in mind when approaching the cards:

- Keep your questions and your spreads simple unless you are prepared for all of the information. Remember, situations are always multilayered and complex; sometimes too many details get in the way.

- Don't be afraid to make up your own spreads so that each reading can be tailored to your individual situation. The Celtic Cross spread doesn't have *all* the answers!

- Sometimes only using the major arcana in a reading can be more useful than the entire deck! Major arcana cards depict the archetypical human experience and can bring exact focus to a situation, especially when you aren't familiar with the nuances of the minor arcana.

- Do a spread for the long road, but check back in when you hit the stoplights. And don't obsess! Trust in the answers and act accordingly.

- A significator is a card that represents something specific. Sometimes we select a significator card to represent ourselves and then select cards that represent the surrounding environment. Find your personal significator card and a significator card for the trouble. That way, when it comes up in related readings, you will always know what to look for.

- Check the book! When reading for ourselves, we can often imprint our own values onto the cards. Checking the book will help keep you honest.

- **Journal about your sessions.** This is imperative and will help to keep you aware of the changes in the situation as well as the way it develops. Being able to reference your readings at a glance can give you long-term insight into the matters at hand.
- **Focus on the movement of the energy within the situation instead of the outcome.** Outcomes change often, so paying attention to the way in which the surrounding energies manifest in the moment will help keep you aware of what is needed to either change the outcome or ensure its fulfillment.

I will be using tarot cards for our sample spreads, but feel free to use any deck of cards you want, from any system. Shuffle your cards a few times before and between readings to clear the energy. Think of what you need to know, and then draw the cards.

ISOLATION SPREAD

Card 1 [left]: Surrounding influence/detail
Card 2 [center]: Main focus
Card 3 [right]: Surrounding influence/detail

This spread should be performed to find out specific information when you are lacking the necessary details to make an appropriate decision or clarify your own intuitive feelings. The more you work with this simple spread, the better your ability to put the pieces together will become. Once you master reading three cards and weaving their meanings together, moving onto larger spreads will be a breeze.

Card 2 is the main focus for this reading. This card represents the central movement, action, person, or scenario that is in play. Cards 1 and 3 are the surrounding influences or details about what is happening in the second card.

TRIPLE ISOLATION SPREAD

Cards 1–3 [bottom row]: Isolation 1

Cards 4–6 [middle row]: Isolation 2

Cards 7–9 [top row, cascading down right side]: Isolation 3

Card 10 [bottom row, far right]: How to move forward

This is the spread I use when I need to get a bird's-eye view of a situation. Essentially, it uses three isolation spreads and then a final card to help provide instruction about what comes next. For this spread, as well as most larger spreads, it is usually a good idea to break down the spread into smaller comprehensive sections. In this case, each isolation will provide us with a clear way of doing that.

Read each of the isolations as you were instructed in the previous exercise. Each isolation represents a situation or movement that is happening now. The tenth card provides you with a little bit of inspiration regarding the best way to move forward.

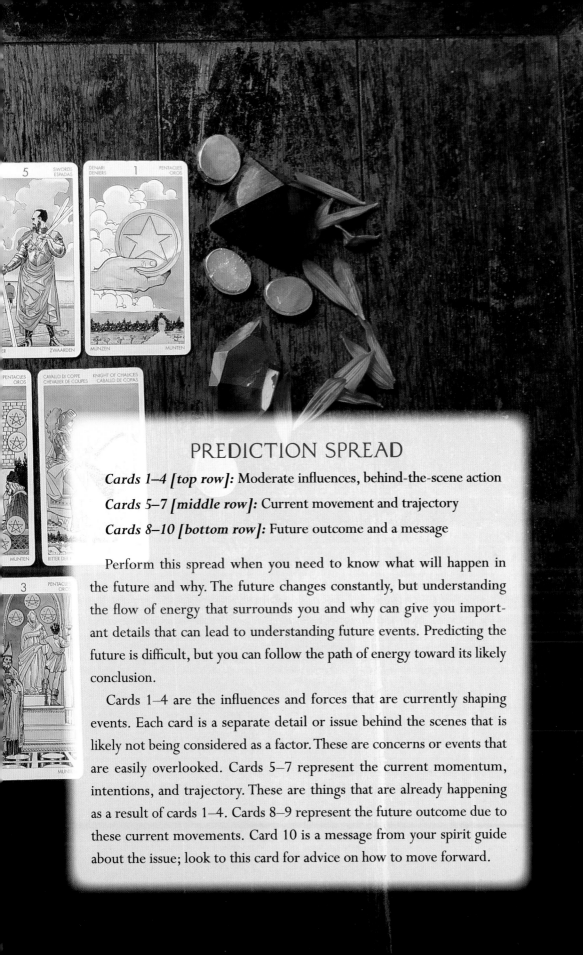

PREDICTION SPREAD

Cards 1–4 [top row]: Moderate influences, behind-the-scene action

Cards 5–7 [middle row]: Current movement and trajectory

Cards 8–10 [bottom row]: Future outcome and a message

Perform this spread when you need to know what will happen in the future and why. The future changes constantly, but understanding the flow of energy that surrounds you and why can give you important details that can lead to understanding future events. Predicting the future is difficult, but you can follow the path of energy toward its likely conclusion.

Cards 1–4 are the influences and forces that are currently shaping events. Each card is a separate detail or issue behind the scenes that is likely not being considered as a factor. These are concerns or events that are easily overlooked. Cards 5–7 represent the current momentum, intentions, and trajectory. These are things that are already happening as a result of cards 1–4. Cards 8–9 represent the future outcome due to these current movements. Card 10 is a message from your spirit guide about the issue; look to this card for advice on how to move forward.

CONCLUSION

We have come to the end of our journey together, but I hope you continue to walk the path we have explored throughout this book. Modern witchcraft is a beautiful menagerie of beliefs and practices, and everyone seeking a place can find a home here. Whether you are a novice in need of a quick magical fix or a seasoned witch who has cast hundreds of spells, my wish is for you to have found something valuable in these pages that you can add to your own practice and that will help make your life better in some way. As we have seen, sometimes big magic comes in small packages or through simple adjustments. No matter how difficult a situation or insurmountable an obstacle may feel, you are never without the resources to seize the day. Magic and witchcraft will always be there to help slay the things that make us feel small.

Love magic can be used to soothe the broken heart or ignite the flames of passion. Healing magic can speed up recovery and banish illness. Protection magic can keep you and your loved ones safe. Prosperity magic can help you rise from mediocrity and say goodbye to financial insecurity. Finally, divination can be used to help navigate the often-murky waters of life so you can see where you are going. In this book we have examined how each of these five types of magic can be woven into our lives, and I have shared personal insights of my own that come from almost two decades of practice. We have done all we can together in this setting. The ball is in your court now, and it is up to you to take what you have learned and do something with it.

Let this book be a guide as you continue to try out new things, experiment with different techniques, and create new magical operations of your own. Revisit it when you have a question, and check out the Modern Witch podcast or *Modern Witch* magazine for more information and resources to help you along the path.

BIBLIOGRAPHY

Anaar. *The White Wand: Towards a Feri Aesthetic*. Self-published, 2005.

Anderson, Victor. *Etheric Anatomy: The Three Selves and Astral Travel*. Albany, CA: Acorn Guild Press, 2004.

Bruce, Robert. *The Practical Psychic Self-Defense Handbook: A Survival Guide*. Charlottesville, VA: Hampton Roads Publishing, 2011.

Buckland, Raymond. *The Spirit Book: The Encylopedia of Clairvoyance, Channeling, and Spirit Communication*. Canton, MI: Visible Ink, 2006.

Cabot, Laurie. *Laurie Cabot's Book of Spells & Enchantments*. Salem, NH: Copper Cauldron, 2014.

———. *Power of the Witch*. NY: Delacorte Press, 1989.

Casey, Caroline W. *Making the Gods Work for You: The Astrological Language of the Psyche*. NY: Harmony Books, 1998.

Cheung, Theresa. *The Element Encyclopedia of the Psychic World*. NY: HarperElement, 2010.

Coyle, T. Thorn. *Evolutionary Witchcraft*. NY: J. P. Tarcher/Penguin, 2004.

Cunningham, Scott. *Cunningham's Encyclopedia of Magical Herbs*. St. Paul, MN: Llewellyn, 1985.

DuQuette, Lon Milo. *My Life with the Spirits: The Adventures of a Modern Magician*. York Beach, ME: Samuel Weiser, 1999.

Farrar, Janet, and Gavin Bone. *Lifting the Veil: A Witches' Guide to Trance-Prophecy, Drawing Down the Moon, and Ecstatic Ritual*. Eugene, OR: Acorn Guild Press, 2016.

Grimassi, Raven. *Italian Witchcraft: The Old Religion of Southern Europe*. St. Paul, MN: Lewellyn Worldwide, 2000.

Harner, Michael. *Way of the Shaman*. San Francisco, CA: Harper & Row, 1980.

Hawkes, Joyce Whiteley. *Resonance: Nine Practices for Harmonious Health and Vitality*. Carlsbad, CA: Hay House, 2012.

Heaven, Ross, and Simon Buxton. *Darkness Visible: Awakening Spiritual Light through Darkness Meditation*. Rochester, VT: Destiny Books, 2005.

Hunter, Devin. *Witch's Book of Mysteries*. Woodbury, MN: Llewellyn, 2019.

———. *Witch's Book of Power*. Woodbury, MN: Llewellyn, 2016.

———. *Witch's Book of Spirits*. Woodbury, MN: Llewellyn, 2017.

Illes, Judika. *Element Encyclopedia of 5000 Spells*. London: Element, 2004.

———. *Element Encyclopedia of Witchcraft*. London: Element, 2005.

Kynes, Sandra. *Llewellyn's Complete Book of Correspondences: A Comprehensive & Cross-Referenced Resource for Pagans & Wiccans*. Woodbury, MN: Llewellyn, 2013.

Leland, Charles G. *Aradia, or, The Gospel of the Witches*. With additional material by Chas Clifton, Robert Mathiesen, and Robert Chartowich. Blaine, WA: Phoenix Publishing, 1998.

———. *Etruscan Roman Remains and the Old Religion*. NY: Kegan Paul, 2002.

———. *Gypsy Sorcery and Fortune Telling*. NY: Citadel Press, 1990.

Liddell, Henry George. *A Greek-English Lexicon*. Oxford, UK: Clarendon Press, 1940.

Madden, Kristin. *Magick, Mystery and Medicine: Advanced Shamanic Healing*. St. Louis, MO: WillowTree Press, 2008.

Melody. *Love Is in the Earth*. Wheat Ridge, CO: Earth-Love Publishing House, 2007.

Miller, Jason. *Sex, Sorcery, and Spirit: The Secrets of Erotic Magic*. Pompton Plains, NJ: New Page Books, 2015.

Parker, Julia, and Derek Parker. *Parkers' Astrology*. NY: DK Publishing, 1991.

Penczak, Christopher. *Spirit Allies: Meet Your Team from the Other Side*. Boston, MA: Weiser Books, 2002.

Smith, Jacki. *Coventry Magic with Candles, Herbs, and Oils*. San Francisco, CA: Red Wheel/Weiser, 2011.

Starhawk. *The Spiral Dance*. NY: Harper One, 1989.

Stephen, Drake Bear. *Soul Sex: The Alchemy of Gender & Sexuality*. Concord, CA: Wisdom Weaver Press, 2015.